# PUTTING YOUR SMALL BUSINESS ON THE WEB

MARIA LANGER

D1364878

PEACHPIT PRESS

# Putting Your Small Business On the Web

Maria Langer

## PEACHPIT PRESS

1249 Eighth Street ○ Berkeley, CA 94710
510/524-2178 ○ 800/283-9444 ○ 510/524-2221 (fax)

**FIND US ON THE WORLD WIDE WEB AT:**
http://www.peachpit.com

Peachpit Press is a division of Addison Wesley Longman
Copyright © 2000 by Maria Langer

**EDITOR** ○ Nancy Davis
**PRODUCTION COORDINATOR** ○ Kate Reber
**COMPOSITOR** ○ Maria Langer
**COVER DESIGN** ○ Earl Gee Design
**COVER ILLUSTRATION** ○ Doug Ross
**INTERIOR DESIGN** ○ Mimi Heft
**INDEXER** ○ Emily Glossbrenner

**COLOPHON**
This book was created primarily with PageMaker 6.5 on a Power Macintosh G3/300 minitower. Screen shots were created with Snapz Pro on an iMac and HiJaak Pro on a Gateway GP6-266, then saved as grayscale TIFFs with Photoshop 5.5.The fonts used were Meta Plus (FontShop), NIMX Quirks (ImageClub), and Missive (T-26). Final output was at Edwards Brothers in Ann Arbor, MI, and it was printed on 50# Arbor Smooth.

ISBN 0-201-71713-1

9 8 7 6 5 4 3 2 1

Printed and bound in the United States of America

To the individuals and businesses of Wickenburg who have
entrusted me to help them build a Web presence, especially:

Dave Waddell of Chrome Caballeros,
http://www.chromecaballeros.com/

Bob and Victoria Nuth of Coldwell Banker Bob Nuth &
Associates, http://www.wickenburgrealestate.com/

Janet LeRoy and Steve Wall of Janet LeRoy, Original Artwork
on Feathers, http://www.wickenburg-az.com/feather/

Max, Sandy, and Katey Conley of Ranch Dressings,
http://www.wickenburg-az.com/ranchdressings/

Peter McMillan and Mark Rebholz of The Vimy Aircraft Project,
http://www.vimy.org/

The members of the Wickenburg Area Merchants Organization
(W.A.M.O.), http://www.wickenburg-az.com/wamo/

# Acknowledgments

I'd like to take this opportunity to thank the people who have made this book what it is.

First, many thanks to Nancy Davis, my long-distance editor. Nancy edits with a light touch and manages to find every little boo-boo my speedy typing fingers make that my own eyes fail to see. Her input on content was extremely valuable.

Next, thanks to Nancy Ruenzel and Marjorie Baer at Peachpit Press for letting me write something new and different. Visual QuickStarts are okay to write, but it's nice to let my hair down and write something fun.

Also, a big thanks to Kate Reber at Peachpit for not nitpicking too much about my layout skills. Hey, I moved those shaded tip bars up three pixels like you wanted, didn't I?

Another big thanks goes out to the Wickenburg-area folks who let me help them put their small businesses on the Web. This book is dedicated to all of you. Best wishes for the twenty-first century!

A special thanks goes out to the Webmasters and Web designers whose sites are mentioned or illustrated on these pages. Thanks for all the hard work you do to make your site what it is.

Finally, thanks to Mike for the usual reasons.


*Maria Langer*
Wickenburg, AZ

July 2000

# Contents

# Part II ○ Building Your Site 71

# Part III ○ Going Online

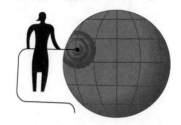

# INTRODUCTION

# Start Here

The Web! Everyone's talking about it, exploring it, "surfing" it. People research products and services and shop there. Now *you* want to join the millions of individuals, businesses, and organizations on the Web by getting your business online.

Although I'm sure you're anxious to start learning the hows and whys of putting your business on the Web, take a moment to read this Introduction. In it, I explain the goals, organization, and conventions of the book. Then I tell you a little about me, so you can start thinking of me as your knowledgeable friend in the Web publishing world.

## In This Introduction

PUTTING YOUR SMALL BUSINESS ON THE WEB

ABOUT THE AUTHOR

# *Putting Your Small Business on the Web*

Watch TV and what do you see? Commercials for e-commerce, Web server solutions, and "dot com" companies. As the public gets more and more familiar with Internet technology, the companies that make technology products and offer technology services are reaching into our living rooms to tell us about them.

For small business owners and managers interested in growing their businesses, these advertisements act as powerful lures, with promises of bigger profits and higher status. These people want to become part of the Web revolution because of what they think it can do for them, based on what they see in the media and hear from consultants looking for work.

Sound familiar? It should. Chances are, you're one of these people.

## About this Book

*Putting Your Small Business on the Web* is a guide to building a Web presence for your business. It explains, in plain English, what the Web can and can't do for your business and how it can be used as an effective marketing tool. It summarizes the costs of building a Web presence and provides a wealth of information about how you can save money with a do-it-yourself approach. If you decide to hire a Web designer, it helps you by explaining how to find the right designer and stay in control of the Web site creation process.

My goal in writing this book is to answer all of the questions my clients have asked throughout the years, and to clear up any misconceptions you may have about the Web as a business tool. Along the way, I provide useful tips and ideas for getting more out of a Web site and saving money.

## Organization

This book is organized into three parts:

## Part I: Overview

The first part of the book provides a lot of basic information about the Internet, including how you can benefit from a Web presence. It also discusses the costs of building and owning a Web site, as well as Web serving options.

Chapter 1: Internet Basics

Chapter 2: What the Web Can—and Can't—Do for You

Chapter 3: What It Costs

Chapter 4: Web Hosting Options

## Part II: Building Your Site

The second part of the book covers the nuts and bolts of building a Web site. It starts with content, interface, and design considerations, then provides information about building the site yourself or finding and working with a Web designer.

Chapter 5: Site Content

Chapter 6: Interface Elements & Features

Chapter 7: Site & Page Design

Chapter 8: Saving Money by Doing It Yourself

Chapter 9: Working with a Web Designer

## Part III: Going Online

The last part of the book explains what you need to put your Web site online and what to do once it's there. It covers uploading your site to the Web server as well as promoting and maintaining your site.

Chapter 10: Uploading Your Site

Chapter 11: Directing Visitors to Your Site

Chapter 12: Maintaining Your Site

### Appendixes

At the very end of the book, you'll find some reference material, including a list of all books and Web sites mentioned within the book. The two appendixes are:

Appendix A: Bibliography

Appendix B: Web Sites & Pages

### Conventions

In addition to plain old text, this book uses a variety of stylistic techniques to communicate special information:

**TIP ▶** *Tips are bits of information that you might find unusually helpful. You can recognize a tip by the Tip icon to its left and the dark, italic type.*

*Pull quotes are supposed to be plain old text that's important enough to be repeated with fancy formatting like this. But I don't like to repeat myself, so I use pull quotes to stress important things.*

**Sidebars**

Sidebars, which have fancy shading, provide supplemental information. I often use sidebars to tell stories or express extremely strong opinions. If a sidebar is very short, it might squeeze into the left column, but usually they're as wide as this one and positioned at the top or bottom of a page.

**NEW TERMS**, when they appear in text, are highlighted by gray bold type. You can find the term defined in a shaded box on the bottom of one of the two pages in front of you—the **PAGE SPREAD**.

There are also plenty of numbered figures with captions and a handful of tables.

### Food for Thought

At the end of each chapter, you'll find a section called "Food for Thought." This is where you'll find suggestions for thinking about the chapter's topics and applying them to your situation. I highly recommend that you go through these little exercises. They'll really reinforce what's covered in the chapter.

## Companion Web Site

Most of my books have companion Web sites, but this book's site is really special—it has its own domain name: smallbusinessonweb.com.

The companion Web site includes a variety of information of interest to readers:

- A message board, with discussions about chapter contents and "Food for Thought" exercises.

- A mailing list, for networking with other small business owners and managers.

- Links to online resources for small business Web publishers.

- Corrections and clarifications for book contents.

You can visit the book's companion Web site at **http:// www.smallbusinessonweb.com/**. And send your friends—I'm sure they'll get something out of it, too.

## Pronouns Shouldn't Come in Pairs

Throughout this book, when I refer to an unspecified person, I use the pronouns *he*, *his*, and *him* instead of *he or she*, *his or her*, and *him or her*. I do this because I think those married pronouns are really distracting, especially when they appear multiple times in a sentence or paragraph.

---

**NEW TERM**
An important word or phrase that is defined in a box like this one.

**PAGE SPREAD**
The two facing pages of a book when it is open.

Why the male pronouns? Well, back when I was in college, I had a marketing professor who was a feminist. He always used the female pronouns—she and her—when he spoke. I found that almost as distracting as the married pronouns, so I don't do that either.

Trust me, I'm not trying to alienate my female readers. And I know they'll understand.

# About the Author

If you're wondering how I qualify to write this book, let me explain with a thorough introduction.

### Who Am I?

I've been working with personal computers since the mid 1980s. In 1990, after an extremely boring career as an auditor and financial analyst (I have a bachelor's degree in accounting), I began a freelance career as a writer, computer consultant, and computer applications trainer. By 1992, I was writing how-to books for popular computer applications. (I've written 28 books since then. You may see estimates of "billions and billions," but it only seems that way.)

I got involved with the Web in 1995 when one of my clients decided to build a Web presence. I learned HTML and started building Web pages. Since then, I've built quite a few Web sites for small businesses, including most of the local Web sites illustrated throughout this book.

My Web work has taught me many things that I think are vital to the success of a small business Web site. It has also helped me develop my own Web authoring philosophy, which is constantly being refined. This is some of the information I'm sharing in this book.

These days, I spend most of my working hours writing computer how-to books and articles and maintaining the Web sites I've built. My labor of love is wickenburg-az.com (**http://www.wickenburg-az.com/**), which I hope you'll find time to visit.

When I'm not working, I'm nowhere near my computer. Instead, I'm usually outdoors (weather permitting; it gets pretty darn hot here in the summer!), working in the garden, horseback riding, motorcycling, off-roading in my Jeep, or flying a helicopter.

## Why I Wrote This Book

I wrote this book for one simple reason: I was sick and tired of seeing small business owners getting ripped off by unscrupulous Web consultants and ISPs. (You'll read some real-life horror stories throughout this book.) I wanted to empower people like you by taking the mystery out of the Internet and Web publishing so you can use them to your benefit.

Let's face it: unless your business is in the computer industry, you probably don't know much about computers. That's fine—you don't have to. But if you want to build a Web presence, you need to understand enough about the process to prevent hungry (or greedy) consultants and ISPs from taking advantage of you.

That's where I can help. I might not be totally objective (I do have my opinions), but I *am* honest. I'll give you the facts and the benefit of my experience. I'm on your side. I'm not trying to sell anything (other than this book, of course), so I'm not motivated to lie or stretch the truth—like the Internet professionals who want your business.

## How You Can Contact Me

I enjoy reading feedback about my work—especially positive feedback. And although I don't *like* to hear about errors, I *need* to hear about them so I can publish corrections on the book's companion Web site, **http://www.smallbusinessonweb.com/**. I depend on you to let me know how I'm doing.

The best way to contact me is via e-mail: maria@gilesrd.com. I get dozens of e-mails a day, so I can't promise a response. But I do eventually read all messages and appreciate the time you've taken to write.

And I hope you can visit me in my virtual home, **http://www.marialanger.com/**. That's where you can learn more about me and the things I do.

# PART I

# Overview

So you're thinking about building a Web presence for your company. Great! But what do you know about the Internet and the people who use it? What do you expect your new Web site to do for you? What do you think a Web site costs to create and maintain? And just how do you expect to get your Web site online?

This part of the book answers all of these questions and more to introduce you to the concept of building a Web presence.

# Part I Table of Contents

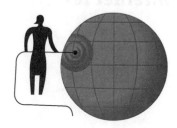

# CHAPTER ONE

# Internet Basics

Unless you're in the computer business or you spend all your free time "surfing the 'Net," you're probably not on intimate terms with the Internet. In fact, you may not even be sure what the Internet is and how it works.

This chapter will clear up any questions you might have about the Internet and World Wide Web by reviewing Internet basics. It also provides some interesting statistics about the people who use the Internet and how they use it.

## In This Chapter

# Internet 101

The Internet has become a part of our lives. We hear about it on the evening news, read about it in the papers, and see references to it in advertising. But exactly what is the Internet? And how does the World Wide Web fit into the picture?

Let's start at the beginning, with an overview of the Internet and the World Wide Web.

## What is the Internet?

The **INTERNET** is a global network of computers.

Imagine a bunch of powerful computers, each located in different cities all over the world. These computers are connected by high-speed network connections, so they can exchange information very quickly. Figure 1.1 shows how such a network might be configured.

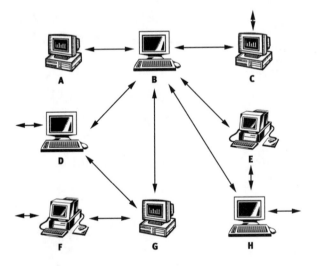

**FIGURE 1.1**
The Internet is a collection of computers connected by high-speed network connections.

These computers are not always directly connected to each other, so sometimes information must pass through one computer to get to another. For example, if Computer A has information that Computer F wants, the information may need to pass from Computer A through Computers B and G on its way to Computer F.

This is how the Internet works: by passing information to a computer that requests it, from a computer that has it. The information can be anything that can be stored on a computer: like an e-mail message, a Web page, a digital picture, or a computer program.

## A Brief History of the Internet

The Internet has been around since the late 1960s. Back then, Cold War fears convinced the U.S. government that its defense computer systems needed protection in the event of a nuclear war. Multiple mainframe computer systems were networked together in such a way that if any one system was destroyed, information could still be shared among the others. This was called DARPAnet (short for Defense Advanced Research Projects Agency network). Later, the D for Defense was dropped, leaving ARPAnet.

In the 1980s, the military sites of ARPAnet split off, leaving behind the research sites. Additional networks—including Usenet and BITNET, were developed and linked to ARPAnet via **GATEWAYS. INTERNET PROTOCOL** (or **IP**) was developed so that each computer on the network could route information to any other computer on the network via the shortest possible route.

In 1986, the National Science Foundation Network (NSFNET) was created. Based around five supercomputers, it enabled researchers to use computer resources without traveling to the computer itself. When linking computers via ARPAnet didn't work out, NSFNET built its own network, which was managed and upgraded by IBM and a number of other companies.

**INTERNET**
A global network of computers linked together for the exchange of information. Also referred to as *the 'Net*.

**GATEWAY**
A network feature that enables information to pass between two different types of networks.

**INTERNET PROTOCOL (IP)**
A set of instructions that enables one computer in a network to know about and exchange information with all other computers in the network.

In 1990, NSFNET replaced ARPAnet, which was dismantled. Other smaller networks also disappeared. Companies began linking their own internal networks to NSFNET, taking advantage of its existing network connections to exchange e-mail and other information. Throughout the world, other networks were linked to NSFNET, building a global network.

In the early 1990s, the U.S. government was funding NSFNET. That stopped in 1995, when NSFNET closed down. Amazingly, the network built around it continued to function, supported by the big organizations that were linked to it—primarily phone companies and America Online. The end result of all this is the commercial Internet we know today.

Nowadays, you don't have to be a big company to connect to the Internet. Anyone with a computer or **INTERNET APPLIANCE** can do it. The Internet is booming and access is getting cheaper, easier, and more reliable all the time. Despite the fact that the Internet isn't owned or controlled by any one individual or organization, it will continue to grow long into the future.

### Internet Features

The Internet offers access to many features. Here are just a few that interest most Internet users:

- **E-MAIL.** Electronic mail makes it possible to exchange written messages with other people all over the world, quickly and cost effectively.

- **SOFTWARE.** FTP (file transfer protocol) makes it possible to exchange computer programs or documents with others, via **UPLOAD** or **DOWNLOAD.**

**INTERNET APPLIANCE**
Any electronic device that can access the Internet. Nowadays, such functionality can be found in many cellular phones, personal digital assistants (PDAs), and televisions.

**UPLOAD**
To send a copy of a computer file from your computer to another computer via modem or network connection.

○ **DISCUSSION GROUPS.** Newsgroups and mailing lists let participants join in topical discussions with people who share their interests.

○ **"PUBLISHED" INFORMATION.** Gopher, WAIS, and World Wide Web servers make it possible to publish and retrieve information from a wide variety of sources.

It's this last feature—published information on the World Wide Web—that has everyone so excited about the Internet. It's the Web that makes the Internet so friendly and useful. And it's the Web that caused rapid growth of the Internet since the mid 1990s.

### Internet vs. Intranet

You may have heard the term **INTRANET** so let me take a moment to explain it.

An intranet is a network that can have the same features as the Internet, but its access is limited to authorized individuals. Think of an intranet as an internal Internet. Many big companies have intranets, which they use to distribute internal information.

Here's an example. I did some Internet-related training for Colgate-Palmolive Corporation several years ago. Its intranet included legal documents, an employee directory, and forms used by the Human Resources and Facilities Management departments. Anyone with access to the intranet can access this information. But although the intranet is connected to the Internet to allow Colgate-Palmolive employees to access Internet information, **FIREWALL** software prevents outsiders from accessing the intranet.

**DOWNLOAD**
To retrieve a copy of a computer file from another computer to your computer via modem or network connection.

**INTRANET**
An internal network with the same features found on the Internet.

**FIREWALL**
Security software that prevents outsiders from accessing the information on an intranet.

# The World Wide Web

The World Wide Web—or simply the Web—is a part of the Internet that provides information, using documents that include one or more of these components:

- **FORMATTED TEXT.** Formatted text makes it more attractive and easier to read and understand. (Well, it's *supposed* to anyway.)

- **IMAGES.** Graphic images make Web information more visually appealing or can provide information that can't be provided with text. Other multimedia elements—including sounds, movies, and even interactive games—can also be found on the Web.

- **HYPERLINKS.** Links enable you to navigate from one piece of information to another with just a click.

- **FORMS.** Fill-in forms enable you to provide information that can be used to find information that interests you (in the case of a search form) or stored in a database (in the case of a database entry form).

*A lot of people think the World Wide Web is the same as the Internet. This isn't true. The World Wide Web is only part of the Internet. The Internet is far more than just the World Wide Web.*

### A [Very] Brief History of the World Wide Web

The Web was created in the early 1990s by Tim Berners-Lee and Robert Cailliau, two members of CERN, a physics research facility in Switzerland. It began as an academic project to make it easier for physicists to share information. Although Gopher, another information publishing feature, was already on the Internet, the formatted text and hyperlinks on **WEB PAGES** made it a more flexible information distribution tool.

The Web was used primarily by these researchers and scientists until around 1993 when NSCA Mosaic hit the scene. Written by

Marc Andreessen (later a founder of Netscape Communications), the Mosaic **Web browser** was stable, available on multiple platforms (other Web browsers were available only for Unix workstations), and free. People—and the media—began to notice the Web. Soon all kinds of organizations, from individuals and clubs to multinational conglomerates, began to publish and access information on the Web.

As the Web began to gain momentum, other Web browsers were developed—notably Netscape Navigator and Microsoft Internet Explorer. "Browser wars" ensued, but that's another story.

Originally, Web documents were based entirely on HTML (hypertext markup language), a system of tags or codes that determines how information in the document looks or behaves. As Web browsers, publishers, and users became more sophisticated, additional languages were added to the Web publisher's toolbox, including DHTML, Java, JavaScript, VRML, and XML. (I discuss all of these Web publishing technologies in Chapter 8.) As a result, there is more control over the appearance of information, more dynamic information, and a greater level of interactivity on the part of the Web user than ever before.

Today, there are billions of Web pages on the World Wide Web. According to some sources, the Web is doubling in size every year, with an estimated 10 million sites as of January 2000. Not bad for a little academic project in Switzerland, is it?

**How the Web Works**

To really understand the Web, you need to know a little about how it works. Although you could sit down with the System Administrator of a big site like Yahoo! or MSN and learn all kinds of technical details about protocols, packets, and proxies, you don't need that level of understanding. (I don't either. In fact,

**Hyperlinks**
Text or graphics you can click to view other information. Hyperlinks are often referred to as just plain *links*. Text links are sometimes called *hypertext links*.

**Web Page**
A document on the World Wide Web. Normally created with HTML, Web pages can be any length and are viewed with Web browser software.

**Web Browser**
A software program used to view and navigate Web documents.

few people do.) Instead, allow me to tell you what you need to know in language we can all understand.

### A Look at the Server

Every Web site lives on a **WEB SERVER**, a computer set up to "serve" Web pages and related information. The Web server has a direct connection to the Internet and a static **IP ADDRESS** that is associated with the Web site's **DOMAIN NAME**. The Web server software runs silently, waiting for requests from Web browsers.

On the server's hard disk are all the documents that make up the Web site. This usually includes HTML documents, images, and multimedia elements. (The server may also include programs called *CGIs* that enable it to perform tasks such as processing forms or searching for data, but we don't need to go into that right now.)

*There are very few cross-platform compatibility issues on the Web. Any kind of computer—Macintosh, Windows (any flavor), or Unix—can serve Web pages to any kind of computer.*

### A Browser Knocks

A Web user accesses the Web using Web browser software. He runs the software and if necessary, the software establishes an Internet connection. The user then tells the Web browser to open a **URL** or Web address.

Every URL has several parts. The first part provides the type of request. For Web pages, this is usually *http*. (In case you're wondering, this stands for *hypertext transfer protocol*.) The second part provides the name of the server. This usually begins with *www*, but doesn't have to. For U.S. sites, this often ends with *.com*, but it can also be *.org*, *.net*, or other dot-letters.

**WEB SERVER**
A computer that is connected to the Internet (or an intranet) and runs software capable of handling HTTP requests.

**IP ADDRESS**
A unique numerical address assigned to a computer on the Internet.

**DOMAIN NAME**
A name associated with an IP address. *peachpit.com* and *wickenburg-az.com* are two examples of domain names.

The last part provides the path and name of the Web page. If this last part is omitted, the **HOME PAGE** is assumed.

**TIP ▶** *You can learn more about URLs in "A Beginner's Guide to URLs" at http://www.ncsa.uiuc.edu/demoweb/url-primer.html.*

When the Web user enters his request, his Web browser begins a conversation with the domain name server he specified in his Internet configuration. It basically says, "What's the IP address for this domain name?" The domain name server searches its database and sends the IP address back to the Web browser. The Web browser can then find the proper Web server and present its request.

### The Web Server Responds

The Web server, which may be busy or idle depending on how active the site is, gets the browser's request. If it can find the requested page, it begins sending the file's data to the Web browser. If the file includes references to other files—such as images—it sends them, too. Each request it handles is referred to as a **HIT**.

If the server can't find the requested page, it sends an error message to the Web browser. You may have seen this as an "Error 404" message.

### The Page Appears

The page begins to appear in the Web browser window. How quickly it appears depends on several factors:

○  How fast is the user's connection to the Internet?

○  How fast is the server's connection to the Internet?

---

**URL (UNIFORM RESOURCE LOCATOR)**
An Internet address that includes the protocol required to open the document. For example, *http://www.wickenburg-az.com/weather/weather.html* is a URL.

**HOME PAGE**
The main entry page of a Web site. Think of this: The home page is to a Web site as a front door is to a house.

**PAGE HIT**
A request for a Web page document. A page hit can result in additional hits to images and other files referenced in the Web page.

- How large are the files that make up the Web page?

- How many requests is the server handling at once?

- How much traffic is on the 'Net, slowing things down?

(Depending on how the server is configured, it can send multiple files at the same time—even to multiple Web browsers—so with fast connections, page elements can pop up quickly.)

### The User Follows a Link

When the user clicks a link on the page, he initiates another request based on the URL embedded in the link. If the request is to a different domain name, the Web browser talks to the domain name server again; if it's to another page on the same site, the request goes straight to the Web server.

### Putting It all Together with an Example

My Web server is a good example. It's a Power Macintosh running WebSTAR Web server software. It has an ISDN connection to the Internet and is assigned the IP address *207.138.23.226*. That address is associated with the domain name *wickenburg-az.com*. All day and night long, WebSTAR is running, waiting for a chance to serve up Web pages.

On the server's hard disk are all the files that make up the wickenburg-az.com Web site, including HTML page files, JPG and GIF image files, and a few PDF document files. (There are even a few plug-ins and CGIs, but we don't need to go into that now.)

Now suppose my brother Norb, who lives in New Jersey, wants to see how the weather is in Wickenburg. Norb launches his Web browser and it connects to the Internet. He enters the URL for the wickenburg-az.com Current Weather page into his Web browser: **http://www.wickenburg-az.com/weather/weather.html**.

Norb's browser contacts the domain name server he specified when he set up his Internet configuration. The domain name server tells the browser that the information it needs can be found at *207.138.23.226*. The browser then contacts the Web server at that address and requests the file named *weather.html* in the folder named *weather*.

My Web server looks for the file and finds it. It begins sending the HTML document. As it sends the file, it sees references to image files that are part of the Web page. It sends those, too. All the while, it's handling other requests for other pages and images. (It keeps pretty busy.)

Although my Web server's connection to the Internet is only 128 **Kbps** (relatively slow as far as servers go), Norb's connection is only 33.6 Kbps. So no matter how fast my server sends files, the fastest they can reach Norb's browser is 33.6 Kbps. (And that's if the 'Net isn't too busy.) Still, the page appears pretty quickly, primarily because it doesn't contain a lot of large graphics. (I tell you more about my Web design philosophy and why I stick to it in Chapter 7.)

# Web Usage

According to a December 1999 Harris Interactive survey (**http://www.harrisinteractive.com/**), more than 50% of U.S. households have PCs and 90% of them use their PCs to go online. Almost half of all adults use PCs at work and, of those people, 79% go online at work. A Nua Internet Surveys report (**http://www.nua.ie/**) for March 2000 estimates that there are 304.4 million people online worldwide. That's a lot of people **SURFING THE 'NET**! And those numbers are growing very quickly.

But who are these people? How much time do they spend online? And what are they doing when they go online?

**KBPS (KILOBITS PER SECOND)**
A unit used to measure connection or transfer speeds. Refers to thousands of bits per second.

**"SURFING THE 'NET"**
Slang phase that means browsing the World Wide Web.

**TIP ▶** *If you're looking for up-to-date statistics about Web usage, here are three good places to start your search:*

- *MyComputer.com's Web Snapshot, http:// websnapshot.mycomputer.com/ (see Figure 1.2)*

- *CyberAtlas, http://cyberatlas.internet.com/*

- *Nua Internet Surveys, http://www.nua.ie/*

### Who Uses the Web

One way to look at who accesses the Web is by demographics. Here are some recent statistics that help describe Web users in the U.S. Keep in mind that Internet usage is growing at an extremely rapid pace; you can see this in the differences in statistics for similar groups on different dates.

- Internet usage by age is as follows: 18 to 24, 17.5%; 25 to 24, 20.8%; 35 to 44, 24.8%; and 45 to 64, 20%. Source: Media Metrix (http://www.mediametrix.com/), December 1999.

- Elderly, poor, or least-educated people are less likely to access the Internet. Only 30% of people over 65 access the Internet, 32% with

**FIGURE 1.2**
MyComputer.com's Web Snapshot is a good source of statistics about Internet users.

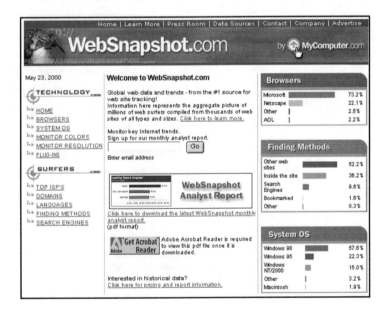

household incomes less than $25,000 access the Internet, and 33% of people who have not completed high school access the Internet. Source: Round Table Group (http://www.round.table.com/), April 2000.

○ Internet usage by white, black, and Hispanic households is about equal with 57% of white and black households having Internet access and 62% of Hispanic households having Internet access. Source: Round Table Group (http://www.round.table.com/), April 2000.

## How Much Time Users Spend Online

A December 1999 Media Metrix survey (http://www.mediametrix.com/) studied Internet access by age:

TABLE 1.1 INTERNET ACCESS BY AGE

| AGE GROUP | TIME ONLINE PER MONTH | UNIQUE PAGE VIEWS PER MONTH |
| --- | --- | --- |
| 18 to 24 | 348 minutes | 385 pages |
| 25 to 34 | 710 minutes | 763 pages |
| 35 to 44 | 617 minutes | 642 pages |
| 45 to 64 | 584 minutes | 564 pages |

What I find especially surprising about these stats is the average amount of time spent viewing each unique page. You can do the math yourself; just divide the number of unique pages by the number of minutes. The answer? About a minute per page. That's not much time to gather information.

A more recent survey by Nielsen/NetRatings, Inc. (http://www.nielsen-netratings.com/) in March 2000 studied Internet access at work and at home:

TABLE 1.2 INTERNET ACCESS AT WORK AND AT HOME

| | AT HOME | AT WORK |
|---|---|---|
| Number of Internet sessions | 19 | 43 |
| Number of unique sites visited per session | 10 | 29 |
| Number of page views per month | 670 | 1,407 |
| Number of page views per session | 35 | 33 |
| Amount of time spent online per month | 9 hrs, 43 mins | 22 hrs, 4 mins |
| Amount of time spent per session | 30 mins | 31 mins |
| Duration of page view | 53 secs | 56 secs |

## How Users Surf

In April 2000, McKinsey and Media Metrix (http://www.mediametrix.com/) released a study that looked at online consumer behavior. The results of the study, titled "All Visitors Are Not Created Equal" separated Web users into six distinct categories:

- ○ **SIMPLIFIERS** are users who access the Internet to make their lives easier. They usually use the Internet for a specific purpose, such as making a purchase or researching a topic. They want to get the job done quickly and easily. On average, these people spend only seven hours a month on the Web, but 49% of them have been using the Internet for at least five years. These people account for more than half of online transactions.

- ○ **SURFERS** are users who access the Internet for many reasons, including entertainment, information, shopping, or just seeing what's out there (exploring). These people account for 8% of Internet users but 32% of online time. They access four times as many pages as the average Internet user and move quickly from site to site, looking for new experiences.

- ○ **CONNECTORS** are relative newcomers to the Internet and are looking for reasons to use it. They make up 36% of Internet users and 40% of them have been online for less than two years. Most of these people use the Internet to communicate with other people via e-mail, chat rooms, and online greeting cards.

○ **BARGAINERS** are users who use the Internet primarily for one purpose: to find bargains. They account for 8% of Internet users and spend less time online than the average user.

○ **ROUTINERS** go online for information. These people spend twice as much time online as the average user, but they visit fewer sites. They spend 80% of their time on "top ten" sites, especially those that provide news and financial information.

○ **SPORTSTERS**, which account for only 4% of Internet users, are basically the same as routiners, but they're more interested in popular sites with sports or entertainment information. They spend only seven hours online each month.

**TIP ▶** *This detailed study goes on to provide specific information about the kinds of sites that attract each group and how organizations can market themselves to them. You can learn more on the press release page for the study: http:// www.mediametrix.com/usa/press/releases/20000417a.jsp.*

Based on this information, I'd have to call myself a simplifier. I use the Internet as a tool for getting my work done, buying things I can't buy locally (heck, I live in Wickenburg, AZ and there isn't much here), and gathering information I need to make decisions.

### Some E-commerce Stats

E-commerce is one area of the Web that's constantly growing. Historically, there were three barriers to e-commerce:

**E-COMMERCE**
Electronic commerce; usually refers to buying and selling on the Web.

- Consumer fears about getting ripped off by the seller.

- Consumer fears about credit card fraud.

- Consumer perception of convenience.

Here are some stats from an April 2000 Angus Reid Group survey (http://www.angusreid.com/) that looked at worldwide online shopping:

- 40% of Internet users have made purchases online.

- 25% of online shoppers have made impulse purchases online.

- 50% of Internet users have researched goods and services online before making offline purchases.

- 93% of online shoppers claimed they were either somewhat satisfied or extremely satisfied with their shopping experience.

- 60% of online shoppers said convenience was the primary reason they shop online.

- A very small percentage of online shoppers said they were concerned about security issues.

# Food for Thought

At this point, you should have a good understanding of what the Internet and World Wide Web are, how they work, who uses them, and how they're used. Now take a moment to think about what you've learned and how you can apply it to your situation.

These questions should help you put things in perspective. To share your answers with others or see what other readers have come up with, visit the book's companion Web site at http://www.smallbusinessonweb.com/.

o   Consider the Internet features listed earlier in this chapter. How
    could you use each of these features to help you expand your
    business or save money (or both)? You'll get some answers to this
    question throughout this book—after all, that's what the book is
    about. But this is a good opportunity to begin thinking of your
    specific situation.

o   Review the discussion of who uses the Internet. Which of these
    groups do your customers fall into? How likely are they to have
    Internet access?

o   Think about the six categories of Internet users covered in the
    McKinsey and Media Metrix survey. Which of the categories do you
    fit into? How about a few of the Internet surfers you know? How do
    you think your Web site could benefit each of these groups?

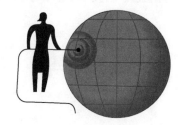

# CHAPTER TWO

# What the Web Can— and Can't—Do for You

Can a Web presence benefit your business? Generally speaking, of course it can! But what kind of benefits can you expect? This chapter lists and explains the benefits of building a Web presence. But it also looks at the other side of the coin to explain what you shouldn't expect from your Web site.

## In This Chapter

WHAT THE WEB CAN DO

WHAT THE WEB CAN'T DO

# What the Web Can Do

No doubt about it, the Web can benefit your business. (That's probably why you're reading this book.) But before you dive into building a Web presence, it's a good idea to know the kinds of things you can expect the Web to do for you.

In this half of the chapter, I give you the good news: a discussion of the things the Web can do for your business, along with real-life examples from businesses like yours.

## Provide Information 24/7

The Web never sleeps. It's available 24 hours a day, 7 days a week, providing the information you think is important to anyone interested in seeing it. This is perhaps the most important yet overlooked feature of the Web, the reason so many people turn to it to answer questions and gather information.

### Look at Me

I'm a good example. I wake up very early (especially in the summer time) and am usually at my desk working by 6:00 AM. Fortunately, the Web is awake and working, too. I can access Web sites for the products I write about and get general information, technical support documents, and even software updates. I can use e-mail links on Web sites to fire off questions and feedback to product marketing people and technical support personnel. I can use forms on Web sites to report problems or request additional information. These are just some of the things I do on the Web.

Now look at the alternative. Say a company I need information about doesn't have a Web site. (Or it has a Web site but the information just isn't there and there's no e-mail contact information.) I have to wait until that company opens for business to call them. (That's if I don't forget; my memory isn't what it used to be.) I may have to deal with an automated phone system that has me pushing buttons for a minute or more. Then I have to hope the person I need information from is available, and, if not, leave a voicemail message and hope he calls me back when I'm available.

By providing the information that people want on a Web site that's available all of the time, you give potential clients, customers, or reviewers a great way to learn what they need to know when they need to know it.

### Example: Coldwell Banker Bob Nuth & Associates
### http://www.wickenburgrealestate.com/

Bob Nuth operates the local branch of Coldwell Banker, a huge real estate company. Although Coldwell Banker has a Web site and offers its branches the ability to include information on its site, Bob wanted a way to reach out to folks looking for real estate in the Wickenburg area, including those folks who never heard of Coldwell Banker.

In deciding on Web site features, Bob assumed that people looking for real estate want to "shop" online—that is, they want to see information about specific listed properties that meet their needs. Although Bob's staff can fax or mail property information to perspective clients, they can't handle requests for information when the office is closed. The Web site, however, can handle requests all the time.

*Online shopping doesn't always involve a purchase or even a purchase decision. Like window shopping, all it requires is something for the shopper to look at and make some basic conclusions about.*

The Coldwell Banker Bob Nuth & Associates Web site provides a searchable database of property listings. The site visitor enters criteria in a search form, then clicks a Search button. A list of properties matching the criteria appears. The site visitor can then click a property link to get details about that property, including (in many instances) a photo (see Figure 2.1). The so-called "property detail" page even includes a lead-generation form that the visitor can fill out if the property interests him.

**FIGURE 2.1**

The Coldwell Banker Bob Nuth & Associates Web site provides a wealth of information about currently available properties, as well as a form the visitor can fill out and send if a property interests him.

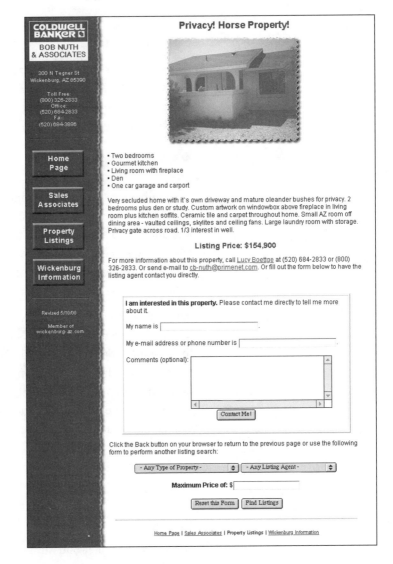

## Reduce Marketing Costs

Once you realize how much information the Web can provide, it isn't hard to imagine how putting marketing information on the Web can save money. What Ben Franklin said in the 1700s still applies today: a penny saved is a penny earned.

*There are two ways to increase your company's net profit or "bottom line": increase revenues or reduce costs. Your company's Web site may not increase revenue by much, but if it cuts costs, the net effect is the same.*

### Marketing vs. Advertising vs. Sales

I want to make some kind of distinction between marketing, advertising, and sales because they are related but different.

Marketing is what you do to attract potential customers and clients and tell them about your products and services. Advertising is part of marketing—getting the word out about your company and what it offers. Sales is the next step: making a deal with the customer or client.

Think of it this way:

o Advertising is standing on a street corner yelling, "Hey! Here I am! Here's what I have to offer!"

o Marketing is saying, "Spend a moment with me so I can tell you how my products and services can benefit you."

o Sales is saying, "Here's the product or service that meets your needs. Here's how much it costs. Will you be paying with cash, check, or charge?"

While this distinction may not seem important now, it will later on in this chapter.

### A Closer Look at Marketing Costs

The money your company spends on marketing can pay for a variety of things. Here are some examples:

o **BROCHURES** show off your products or describe your services in the most enticing terms. You probably want them to look impressive so the people who see them think the best of your company. But impressive brochures can cost lots of money—for layout and design, writing, photography, and printing (especially if done in full color). But what do you do if you add or discontinue a product or service featured in your brochure? Time to get the brochure production team back together!

- ○ **CATALOGS**, like brochures, enable you to show off your products. But they're usually bigger and can be costlier to produce, primarily because they include detailed information about each item. They may also include pricing. While it's great to have a big fat catalog filled with product information and pricing, what happens when the prices change? Throw out the old catalogs and print up some new ones!

- ○ **DIRECT MAIL** is possibly the most costly marketing method. It requires not only printed materials, but a mailing list, prepared labels, and postage. The more information you send out, the more it costs to send. And you're never quite sure if the people who get those direct mail pieces will look at them.

- ○ **PRINT ADS** spread the word about your products or services in a relatively cost-effective way. By placing ads in the newspapers or magazines your market is most likely to read, you can reach potential customers. But the bigger, flashier, and more colorful the ad, the more it will cost. And what if your product or service can appeal to anyone? Which publication do you advertise in? All of them?

- ○ **PENS, MUGS, TEE SHIRTS, AND OTHER HANDOUTS** are a great way to put your organization's name in front of potential customers or clients. They're also a great way to reward current customers or clients. But they cost money and need to be designed so you get your money's worth.

I'm sure you can think of other examples of marketing techniques that cost money. If you're really smart and have a good imagination, you may even think of a few that are free (or almost free).

### Example: Chrome Caballeros Tours
http://www.chromecaballeros.com/

Dave Waddell's motorcycle tour business, Chrome Caballeros Tours, takes all the trouble out of motorcycle camping by carrying all the gear and doing all the work for you. His clients simply ride at their own pace through some of the best scenery the Southwest has to offer and let Dave and his team take care of the rest.

Dave described all this in a professionally produced brochure. But he realized that his growing business would be offering different tours on different dates and at different prices every year. A schedule that was up-to-date today would be out-of-date in a month. So he decided to keep schedule details out of his brochure and provide them on the Web (see Figure 2.2).

Dave's Web site is referenced on all his printed literature— business cards, brochures, letterhead, print ads, and even the big banner he hangs from his support vehicle in camp. When someone calls asking for information, he points them to the Web site before offering to mail out a brochure. In many cases, that's all the caller needs. Dave saves on postage and printing and potential clients get the information they want within minutes. In addition, his Web site can provide up-to-date information about upcoming tours, availability, and pricing.

### Example: Janet LeRoy, Original Artwork on Feathers
http://www.wickenburg-az.com/feather/

Janet LeRoy is an artist who paints wildlife, Native Americans, and other western themes on turkey feathers. Her work, which is finely detailed and embellished with semi-precious stones and rare bird feathers, has to be seen to be fully appreciated.

Janet sells both original pieces and limited edition prints. The prints are available at wholesale prices to galleries, gift shops, and other retailers. Her selection of prints is constantly changing as old prints sell out and new ones are produced.

FIGURE 2.2
The Chrome Caballeros Tours Web site includes a full-color online brochure with up-to-date schedule and pricing information.

Like most artists, Janet is on a tight budget. Printing and mailing out a full-color brochure or catalog every month or so is simply too costly. So Janet turned to the Web to show off her work. Her online gallery of available prints shows thumbnail photographs of each piece (see Figure 2.3). A site visitor can click a thumbnail to view a larger image. Pricing and contact information is right on the Gallery page, making it easy for customers to place orders.

## Reduce Support Costs

If you sell a product or provide a service that requires support, providing that support will keep your customers and clients

**FIGURE 2.3**
Janet LeRoy's Web site includes an online gallery of her available work. These color illustrations can change as often as she needs them to.

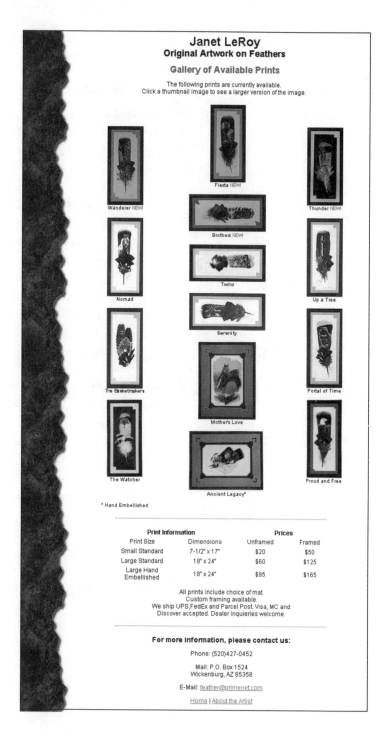

## Janet LeRoy
### Original Artwork on Feathers

### Gallery of Available Prints

The following prints are currently available.
Click a thumbnail image to see a larger version of the image.

Fiesta NEW!

Wanderer NEW!

Thunder NEW!

Brothers NEW!

Nomad

Twins

Up a Tree

Serenity

The Basketmakers

Portal of Time

Mother's Love

The Watcher

Proud and Free

Ancient Legacy*

* Hand Embellished

| Print Information | | Prices | |
|---|---|---|---|
| Print Size | Dimensions | Unframed | Framed |
| Small Standard | 7-1/2" x 17" | $20 | $50 |
| Large Standard | 18" x 24" | $60 | $125 |
| Large Hand Embellished | 18" x 24" | $95 | $165 |

All prints include choice of mat.
Custom framing available.
We ship UPS, FedEx and Parcel Post. Visa, MC and Discover accepted. Dealer inquieries welcome.

### For more information, please contact us:

Phone: (520)427-0452

Mail: P.O. Box 1524
Wickenburg, AZ 85358

E-Mail: feather@primenet.com

Home | About the Artist

loyal. You can save money by using the Web to provide support, even when staff is unavailable.

### The Cost of Support

To get an idea of what you can save by offering Web-based customer support, you need to know some of the costs of providing support. Here are a few of the costs you may already be incurring:

o   **SUPPORT PERSONNEL** are folks that sit around waiting for the phone to ring. When a call comes, they answer questions. The more people you have, the more your personnel costs are. But if you don't have enough of these people, your customers will have to wait too long for answers to their questions. (And those poor support people won't get any rest at all!) Some balance needs to be made. And what if you want to provide 24/7 support? What will those support people be doing in the middle of the night when they only get one or two calls per hour?

o   **TELEPHONE SYSTEMS** are required to connect your customers or clients to your support staff. Depending on the size of your staff, the system you need could be very costly indeed. And if your company generously offers toll-free telephone support, add in the cost of all those toll-free calls. Whew!

o   **FAX-BACK AND FAX-ON-DEMAND SYSTEMS** offer another way of getting support information to customers or clients. These systems can also be costly, especially if the system calls the customer's fax machine to send the information.

o   **MANUALS, USER GUIDES, AND TECHNICAL NOTES** are documents you pay writers like me to produce. (And some of us don't come cheap.) Preparing these documents is only part of the cost— printing and distributing them adds to the cost. And if you decide to include only the basic manuals with your product, you might find yourself mailing or faxing more advanced documents to the people who need them. That increases costs, too.

○ **UPDATES** are revisions that make your product work better. They're especially common in the computer industry, where software products are often released before they're ready and bug-fixes are required. But other products—or product manuals—could require updates, too. In most cases, you'll want your customers to get updates because they can solve problems customers may already have.

### Example: TriGeo, Inc.
### http://www.trigeo.com/

TriGeo, Inc. is a small Idaho-based company that develops and sells weather, Internet, mapping, and environmental software. It also acts as a retailer for weather stations, which it bundles with its software at competitive prices.

TriGeo may be small, but it's big on technical support. Its management understands that in a narrow yet competitive market, providing good technical support can make the company stand out. (It certainly worked for me; I bought my weather station and software from them after their prompt and friendly responses to my pre-purchase questions.)

TriGeo doesn't have a big staff or a fancy telephone system. Instead, it provides a wealth of technical support information on its Web site. The main support page (see Figure 2.4) offers links to pre-purchase support documents, such as product briefs, as well as post-purchase support documents, such as user manuals, application notes, and **FAQs**. The same page also includes telephone and fax numbers and an e-mail address for technical support personnel—just in case you don't get your answer on the Web site. TriGeo promises to call you back within one business day and they haven't broken that promise to me once yet.

**FAQ (FREQUENTLY ASKED QUESTION)**
A list of questions and answers often asked by customers. Answering questions before they're asked is a good way to minimize support costs.

**FIGURE 2.4**
The TriGeo, Inc. support page includes
links to many support documents.

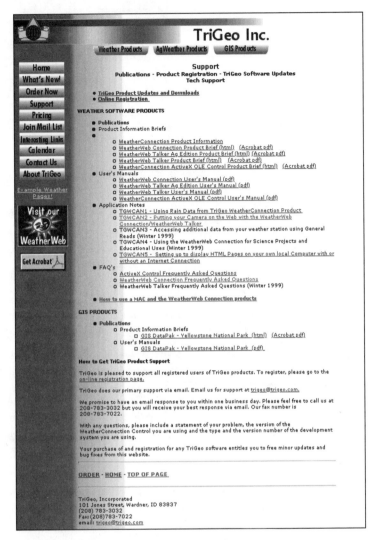

## Give Your Organization a More Modern Image

If your business has been around for a long time, you may
already have success with traditional methods of marketing,
spreading information about your products or services, and
providing customer support. Great! But you may also realize that
although the old-fashioned way of doing business may work, it
also may look...well, *old fashioned*.

A Web presence *can* help make your company look more modern and up-to-date. Just put a "dot-com" after your business name and throw around your e-mail address, and folks will realize that your business has moved with the rest of the world into the 21st century. But if this is the only reason you want a Web presence, take some time to think about whether that's enough of a benefit to justify the costs.

## Make Your Company Look Impressive or Important

Like a fancy office with expensive furniture, a nicely designed Web site can make you look good to potential customers or clients. But you can take this concept a step further if the site also includes positive product reviews, customer praise, or examples of your best work. It shows your company off, making it look impressive or important to visitors. If done right, it can even make your company look bigger or better than it is.

### Example: The Chicago Safe Company
**http://www.chicagosafe.com/**

C.A. Hall owns and operates The Chicago Safe Company, which is based in Phoenix, AZ. (The name is a long story; don't ask.) C.A. has been in the business for years and has designed and installed standard and custom safe solutions in banks, businesses, and homes all over the United States.

Although a sole proprietorship, The Chicago Safe Company's Web site (see Figure 2.5) is professionally designed, using images that seem to make the company look big, professionally run, and...well, *safe*.

### The Other Side of the Coin

Of course, a poorly designed, amateurish, or incomplete Web site can have the opposite effect on your company's image. Unfortunately, most low-budget or home-grown Web sites fall into this category. These sites do more harm than good. The way I see it, if you can't do it right, don't do it at all.

**FIGURE 2.5**
The Home page for The Chicago Safe Company seems to make the company look enormous.

# What the Web Can't Do

So far, the situation looks good. A Web presence can save you money, enable you to improve marketing and customer service, and give your company the dot-com address it needs to look modern. Contrary to popular opinion, however, a Web presence cannot perform miracles for every company that builds one.

### Beware of Promises Made by Web Consultants

One of the reasons I wanted to write this book is to warn people about Unscrupulous Web Consultants (we'll call them UWCs, for short). These are people who prey upon business managers who know little or nothing about the Web and rely on consultants for all of their information.

A UWC will tell potential clients *anything* to get the contract—even lies. Then, with the client's deposit in hand, the UWC will do whatever he thinks is best to make his portfolio of Web sites look impressive to future clients, regardless of whether it meets the current client's needs. Throughout the process, the client is kept in the dark about almost everything the UWC handles. And, at the end of the process, when the site is online, the client is handed a big bill for services rendered. Monthly or quarterly bills for management services rendered may also appear as long as the site remains online.

I've seen many people burned by UWCs and it makes me angry. Throughout this book, you'll find some of the UWC horror stories I've heard so you can get angry, too. But I'll also provide plenty of do-it-yourself information and tips for finding and working with Web consultants or designers so you don't have to worry about becoming a UWC's victim.

Please don't think every Web consultant or designer is of the unscrupulous variety. Most aren't. But in an ocean full of fish, there are always a few sharks. Don't let a shark get you.

This half of the chapter gives the bad news about a Web presence—a discussion of the things it can't do for you.

## Replace All Other Marketing Tools

Even if you have a Web site, you cannot expect it to replace all other kinds of marketing. Why? Hmm...maybe you should go back and read Chapter 1.

### Flashback to Chapter 1

Back in Chapter 1, I provided lots of stats about the number of people who use the Web and the ways they use it. You should have come away from that discussion with many conclusions, including these two:

o   Not everyone has access to the Web.

o   Not everyone uses the Web to look for businesses like yours.

So even if you believe (for whatever reason) that all of your potential customers or clients access and use the Internet, making the first point moot, you're still zapped by the second point.

### Look at Me (Again)

Although it's embarrassing to admit, I'm an example. I'm literally connected to the Internet all day long when I'm at my desk. My Web browser is always running. I'm constantly switching to it to look up a Web site I need to access for information.

Yet when I was trying to find a Japanese soaking tub like I'd seen in a friend's house years ago, I visited the Home Depot, looked in plumbing catalogs, and asked construction contractors. No one knew what I was talking about; half of them tried selling me a garden tub.

Then a friend of mine asked, "Did you search the Internet?" Duh. I felt like slapping myself on the side of the head. I searched and after wading through an awful lot of junk, found *exactly* what I was looking for. (Now if only I could get the darn thing shipped from Seattle to Wickenburg for less than $400.)

The point is, even the most active Internet user doesn't always turn to the Web to locate products or services.

### Example: Custom Arizona Tours

In late 1999, Joe Smith (a fake name) started a tour business called Custom Arizona Tours (a fake name). Joe, an experienced tour guide who has lived in Arizona most of his life, creates custom tours of Arizona and the southwest for individuals and groups. His clients tell him what interests them and Joe takes care of all the details. Then he comes along on the tour and acts as guide, ensuring that the client's experience is everything they expected and more.

Joe decided that his business's marketing would rely on a Web site to provide information about his services. He put together the kind of information that would appear in a brochure, along with some nice color photographs of Arizona scenery and himself. The Web designer created a simple yet professional-looking Web page and put it on the Web.

Then Joe sat back and waited for the phone to ring. Last time I spoke to him, he was still waiting.

You see, although there's nothing wrong with putting brochure information on the Web, unless people know it exists or where to find it, it probably won't be seen. Joe argues that Web surfers should be able to find his site using search engines. I'm sure some surfers do. But what about the others who don't even look? The ones who rely on travel agents, magazines, and state tourism bureaus for their vacation planning information? And the ones who don't access the Internet at all? Joe will never reach them unless he advertises in other places.

And yes, Joe and his company do exist. But I wouldn't want to embarrass him by putting real names in this book. I just hope he reads this, recognizes himself, and gets the message. And I hope you get the message, too.

## Make Money (with Some Exceptions)

Lots of people think that building a Web site with an online shopping feature is like opening up a store in a popular mall in a wealthy neighborhood. Despite the rather rosy picture painted about e-commerce near the end of Chapter 1, it just ain't so. In fact, huge companies based on e-commerce are having trouble surviving.

### The Big Guys Can't Even Do It

In April 2000, I happened to spend a few nights in a hotel. *USA Today* was on my doorstep every morning. I'm a stat lover and *USA Today* is the newspaper of stat lovers. So I read it.

The April 26, 2000 issue had a great article titled "Cash Clock is Ticking." (You may still be able to find it at **http://www.usatoday.com/life/cyber/invest/in622.htm**.) The article listed 14 **E-RETAILERS** that are publicly traded on one of the major stock exchanges, along with the cash on hand, fourth quarter loss ("cash burned"), and the number of months until cash runs out at the current burn rate for each company. By the time you read this, it's likely that several of the companies listed will be history. In fact, only one was listed as profitable: eBay—and it doesn't even sell its own products! Even the mighty Amazon.com continued to operate at a loss as of the end of 1999.

The point is, if big companies with lots of development and marketing resources can't even make it work, what are the chances that you'll succeed?

Don't get me wrong—I'm not saying that you shouldn't include an online shopping feature on your Web site *if it's applicable to your business*. I'm saying that you shouldn't depend on it for all your sales or even expect it to make a huge impact in your bottom line.

**E-RETAILER**
A retail organization which sells much, if not all, of its products via the Internet.

### Online Store ≠ Traditional Store

An online store isn't the same as a traditional store. There are certain disadvantages to buying online—either actual or perceived:

- One of the reasons that online stores don't always work is the "touchy-feely" aspect. Let's face it—you can show a hundred pictures of your product and describe it in a thousand words. But there are still people out there who like to pick up the product and look at it before they buy it. Unless they've already seen and handled the item elsewhere, they're not going to buy. It's the whole browsing part of shopping, the part that makes it fun (for some people, anyway).

- Some people continue to have fears about trusting an online shopping system with their credit card information. They think that some hacker is going to steal their credit card number and use it to go on a shopping spree or a vacation in Brazil. The truth of the matter is, you're more likely to be a victim of credit card fraud when paying a restaurant bill via credit card than by using your credit card to place an order on a secure, online system. But try telling that to the worry warts who get all their information from the evening news on TV.

- Many people won't buy online simply because it's more convenient or cheaper to buy in a traditional store. After all, why wait until next week to receive a product when they can take a ten-minute drive and buy it immediately? And why pay for shipping? (Of course, depending on the item, the amount of money you save in sales tax could cover the cost of shipping, but some people don't see that either.)

### People Don't Pay for Online Information

Many people think they can build a Web site and make money by charging a fee to access its information. What they don't realize is that the vast majority of people who access the Internet are not willing to pay for the information they receive online. Why? Because there's a good chance they can find the information for free elsewhere.

I am part of this vast majority. I won't pay to access any Web site because, in most cases, I can find the information on another, free Web site. If I can't find it, I convince myself that I don't need it. (I can be pretty convincing.) It's not because I'm cheap; it's because I'm of the old school that believes information on the Internet *should* be free.

### The Exceptions

There are exceptions to every rule and this rule is no exception. (Pun intended; I'll be really surprised if my editor leaves that sentence alone.) The best way to explain is with examples.

Say you've written and published a book about how to build chicken coops. Your book has been reviewed by numerous farm-related publications and everyone is raving about it. You can't get it into the big bookstores (they don't think there's enough of a market) so you decide to sell the book via your Web site. You place ads in the marketing publications chicken farmers (and chicken farmer wannabes) read, inviting them to your Web site to learn more and order online. (Since you know that not everyone is on the Internet, you also provide a phone number or address for orders.) Because you're the only source of the book and it is in demand, you'll probably succeed at selling it. If you're lucky, you'll get a few chicken supply stores interested and they'll place wholesale orders. Maybe you won't make as much per book, but you'll sell more books.

Or say you're a productivity consultant and you spend most of your time conducting research on the impact of color on office productivity. Each month, you publish a newsletter with conclusions from your most recent studies. You can publish it in print or you can make it accessible on your Web site for a fee. If you're well known in your field and your newsletter is in big demand (and someone else hasn't done the same research and published it for free elsewhere), people will pay to access it.

These are just two examples. They have one thing in common: they offer a product or service that is in demand (because of other publicity or marketing efforts) and cannot be gotten elsewhere. Do your products or services meet this criteria? If so, your e-commerce efforts may succeed.

# Food for Thought

Ready to give the topics in this chapter a bit more thought and apply them to your situation? Use these suggestions as a guide. If you'd like to share your ideas with others or see what other readers had to say, visit the book's companion Web site, http://www.smallbusinessonweb.com/.

- What information is important to your customers or clients? Make a list of the topics you can include on your Web site. Remember, the more questions you answer on your site, the fewer questions you'll have to answer by phone, fax, e-mail, or snail-mail.

- Think about your company's marketing costs. If possible, list them, including the annual amount spent on each one. How many of these items could be reproduced on the Web? How many could be complemented with information on a Web site?

- Now think about your company's support costs. If possible, list them, including the annual amount spent on each one. How many of these costs could be reduced by putting them on the Web?

- Do you think your current marketing efforts could help drive visitors to your Web site? What else could you do to generate interest in your site?

- If you're considering e-commerce to sell products or services, list the features of your product or service that make it stand out from the competition. Why would someone be willing to buy it from your Web site?

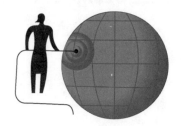

# CHAPTER THREE

# What It Costs

Whether you're trying to decide if the benefits of a Web presence are worth the costs or you've already decided and are just trying to budget for your Web site, it's important to consider *all* costs. This chapter lists and defines the costs related to building and maintaining a Web site, from site design to day-to-day maintenance.

## In This Chapter

SITE DESIGN & CONSTRUCTION

SITE SETUP & HOSTING

SITE MAINTENANCE

ADDITIONAL FEES & HIDDEN COSTS

# Site Design & Construction

The cost of designing and building your Web site can be either the smallest or largest cost of establishing a Web presence. Two factors directly influence costs:

- **WHAT DO YOU WANT TO INCLUDE ON YOUR WEB SITE?** This includes the quantity and quality of content, as well as Web site features such as search capabilities, feedback forms, and counters.

- **WHO WILL DESIGN AND BUILD THE SITE?** You can tackle the job yourself, use or hire an in-house person, or use an outside consultant.

Chapters 5 and 6 cover Web site content, interface elements, and features in detail, so I won't discuss them here. Instead, I'll concentrate on the "who factor" to fully explain your options and give you an idea of related costs.

## Do It Yourself

The do-it-yourself approach can be the least expensive by far. But do you have what it takes to design and build a Web site? And can you afford to spend the time and effort to do the job right? If the answer to either of these two questions is no, the do-it-yourself approach can wind up being quite costly.

### The Right Stuff

To design and build a Web site, you need to have certain skills and knowledge:

- **DESIGN SKILLS** enable you to come up with a design that not only looks good on screen, but is appropriate for your business. Without these skills, your Web site could appear ugly or amateurish or fail to communicate the right image for your company.

- **WEB KNOWLEDGE** gives you an understanding of how text, graphics, and links work on the Web. Without this knowledge, you won't know how to create effective layouts, image displays, or site navigation systems.

○ **WEB AUTHORING SKILLS** makes it possible to turn the design you've developed into a fully-functioning Web site. Without these skills, you won't be able to translate your design into a Web site.

○ **WEB ADMINISTRATION KNOWLEDGE** enables you to upload Web site contents to a Web server, troubleshoot problems, and update pages when necessary. Without this knowledge, you won't be able to get your site online or keep it running smoothly.

If you lack the necessary skills or knowledge to design and build a Web site, you'll have to either learn these skills or hire someone to help you (or, worse yet, fix the mistakes you made). That's going to cost time and money—perhaps the same amount of money you thought you'd save by doing it yourself.

*In general, amateurs build amateurish Web sites. Want proof? Go to http:// hometown.aol.com/and follow the links under Explore Member Pages.*

**TIP ▸** *If you think you have what it takes to design and build a Web site, Chapter 8 is for you! It provides a wealth of information for do-it-yourselfers.*

### Time is Money

Did you ever stop to think about how doing your job affects your company's bottom line? If you're in sales, you may be able to estimate the amount of revenue you generate. You might be able to do the same for other positions. But even if you can't estimate how much you earn for your company, can you estimate what it would cost your company if you couldn't do your job? Because you were, perhaps, busy building a Web site?

Before you start thinking about how much you can save by doing it yourself, take a moment to think about how much it'll cost your company if you weren't doing your usual job. If you're valuable to your company in your current role, perhaps that's the role you should stick to, for the good of the company.

As for building a site in your free time: do you *really* want to do that?

*If your company can benefit more from you doing your regular job than from you spending time building a Web site, you probably shouldn't be building a Web site.*

### Use an In-House Person

The next step up on the expense ladder is using an in-house person to design and build your Web site. For this, you need a person who has the skills and knowledge required to do the job right: a real Web developer.

There are several benefits to using an in-house Web developer:

- In general, in-house Web developers are less expensive than consultants with the same skills and knowledge.

- An in-house Web developer can do all work on your premises, so you can supervise the work and provide input and feedback at any time.

- When the Web site design and construction is finished, an in-house Web developer will be around to troubleshoot and update the Web site when necessary.

Of course, not all businesses need an employee dedicated to designing and building a Web site. For example, if your company plans to build a site that has a lot of general information that does not change, the Web developer probably won't have much to do when the site is up and running. Or if your company is very small, it might not be able to afford an employee for just one job. In either case, it might be more practical to make the Web development task part of an existing job description. Just make sure that the person who does the job has the skills and knowl-edge required to do it right.

### Use a Consultant

The most costly alternative is usually to hire a Web consultant. These people have all the skills and knowledge necessary to get the job done. Hopefully, they also have the communication skills necessary to understand what you want so they can deliver it.

Most consultants charge by the hour. Rates can be anywhere from $20 or $30 per hour up to $150 or $200 per hour. Some consultants charge a per-page fee of anywhere from $20 to $100 per page. (This doesn't make much sense when you consider that a Web page can be any length.) Still other consultants will take on a job at a flat fee. That fee can be considerable—for example, the three pages in The Chicago Safe Company's Web site (http://www.chicagosafe.com/; see Figure 3.1) cost $2,000 to produce. Ouch!

I'd like to say that you get what you pay for, but unfortunately that isn't always true. You can find very reasonable Web consult-ants that do a great job or you can get burned by an expensive Web consultant that doesn't deliver what you want. But if you select the right Web consultant, you'll get a professionally prepared Web site without the bother of doing it yourself or using an in-house developer.

**TIP ▶**  *Back in Chapter 2 there's a sidebar warning about Web consultants. If you skipped over that, read it now. And be sure to read Chapter 9 before you hire a Web consultant.*

# Site Setup & Hosting

Once the site has been designed and built, it needs to be hosted on a Web server. Again, the cost varies depending on choices you make.

## What's In a Name?

There are two ways to set up the URL for your your Web site: as a **SUBSITE** of an existing domain or as a custom domain name. Each has its own pros and cons.

### Being a Subsite

When you're a subsite of an existing domain, your Web site's URL begins with the other domain name. For example, Spirit Riders' Web site (http://www.wickenburg-az.com/spiritriders/) is a subsite of the wickenburg-az.com Web site.

This is, by far, the least expensive way to address your Web site. In fact, many **INTERNET SERVICE PROVIDERS (ISPs)** allow you to create your own subsite on their server for no additional charge.

There are several drawbacks to being a subsite:

○ Having a subsite URL is less impressive than having your own domain name. It's cheaper and anyone can do it, so what's the big deal, right?

○ A subsite URL is longer than a custom domain name. That means it takes longer to read (or spell) to someone and longer to type in.

○ A subsite URL may contain unusual characters, such as the tilde (~). My first Web site's URL included this character and it was a royal pain to read to someone over the phone.

○ A subsite URL is not portable. This means that if you have a falling out with your ISP and want to move your Web site to another server, your URL will change to indicate your new ISP's domain name. This means you'll have to change your URL everywhere it appears—brochures, business cards, letterhead, print ads, etc.

**SUBSITE**
A Web site that is part of another Web site.

**INTERNET SERVICE PROVIDER (ISP)**
An organization that offers access to the Internet, either via dial-up (modem) connection or direct network connection.

I'm not trying to talk you out of setting up your Web site as a subsite. It's a perfectly good solution for families and very small businesses that add a Web site as an afterthought. It's also a good solution for businesses that are part of a larger business—for example, the local office of a nationwide real estate firm.

But for independent businesses that are serious about building a Web presence, having a custom domain name is a much more professional and practical solution.

### Having Your Own Domain Name

When you have your own domain name, your site's URL is usually *http://www* followed by the domain name. For example, http://www.marialanger.com/ and http://www.wickenburg-az.com/ are two examples of URLs for domain names I maintain: marialanger.com and wickenburg-az.com.

Having your own domain name is more expensive than being a subsite. There are at least two specific costs to consider:

- **DOMAIN NAME REGISTRATION FEES** are the costs to register your domain name with the **DOMAIN NAME SYSTEM**. You can register with a number of different organizations. The one that's been around the longest is Network Solutions (**http://www.networksolutions.com**/; see Figure 3.2), which charges $35 per year. If you don't already have an ISP or Web server lined up to host your Web site, you may pay an additional fee to "reserve" the name; Network Solutions charges $5 per year for this service.

- **DOMAIN HOSTING FEES** are the costs to host your domain name on an ISP's server. Because more resources are required to host a domain name than subsite, most ISPs charge a monthly, quarterly, or annual fee for this service. Fees range from about $20 to $100

**DOMAIN NAME SYSTEM (DNS)**
A database of domain names and corresponding IP addresses. All domain name servers have access to this database.

## Network Solutions

At the risk of sounding like a paid advertisement (which this is not), I'd just like to take a moment to talk about the services available at Network Solutions.

I've known Network Solutions since the days it was known as Internic and you needed to be an Internet geek to understand the domain name registration process. In those days, it was the only game in town and *everyone* used it to register domain names. Since then, a number of companies have been authorized to register domain names with the Domain Name System. The addition of competition has benefited the public. Not only can you find a few cheaper domain name registration organizations, but some organizations (including Network Solutions) now offer additional services (for a fee) to help you promote your Web site. (I discuss promoting your Web site in Chapter 11, so don't get all excited about it now.)

In the case of Network Solutions, the biggest benefit of increased competition is the improvements to the domain name registration process. I can now safely say that the process is user friendly. In fact, I'd even bet real money that my mother could register a domain name if she wanted to—and she's the true test of whether a system can be used by the masses.

Want to know if a domain name you're considering has already been taken? Visit Network Solutions at http://www.networksolutions.com/ (see Figure 3.2), enter the domain name (without the w's) in the yellow search box, choose a domain from the menu, and click Go.

FIGURE 3.2

The Network Solutions Web site makes it easy to register a domain name.

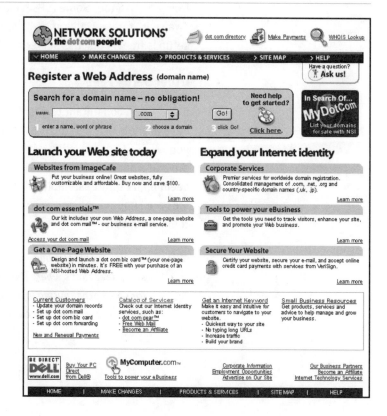

per month, depending on the ISP and its services. If you have your own Web server, these fees may not apply.

The main benefit of having your own domain name is that your Web site's URL can be easily identified (and remembered) as part of your company. But what some people don't consider is the portability of a domain name—you don't need to change your site's URL if you move your Web site to another ISP's server. Since a domain name is like a pointer to a specific IP address, changing the IP address in the Domain Name System automatically updates the domain name to the new IP address. So a Web site move is completely transparent to Web site visitors.

### Server Setup

If you plan to host your Web site on an ISP's server, the ISP may charge a setup fee for the site. This is a one-time fee that ranges from $25 to $100. Some ISPs have a stated fee but generously "waive it" for new customers. (My question: why not just say setup is free?) I discuss server-related fees in Chapter 4.

### Other Setup Fees

If you hire a consultant to design and build a Web site, he may have a whole list of setup fees that you'll have to pay before your Web site goes online. Make sure you know what these fees are and what they cover before you hire the consultant. If they seem high or unreasonable, discuss them. Since many of these fees are simply icing on the cake, you can probably get some of them reduced.

**TIP ▶** *The fee that really bugs me is the so-called domain name setup fee. That's where the consultant charges you $150 (or some other outrageous figure) to register your domain name—something you can do yourself for $35!*

### Web Hosting

Web hosting costs refer to the fees you'll pay to have your site hosted on a Web server. The fees vary based on the hosting options you select. There are so many hosting options that I've written a whole chapter about them: Chapter 4. Be sure to read it and include the costs that apply to you when coming up with a total for the cost of your Web presence.

# Site Maintenance

Even after you design and build your site and get it online, the costs continue. After all, you have to maintain your site so it works properly and remains up-to-date.

This is where your Web developer—whether it's you, an in-house person, or a Web consultant—will be kept relatively busy. The costs, therefore, will be related to the cost of that person.

What does maintenance include? Here are a few things that I do every day/week/month on the Web sites I maintain:

- **ADD FRESH CONTENT.** By far, this is the most time-consuming chore. Only by adding new information can you keep your site interesting to repeat visitors. On one of my sites (wickenburg-az.com), I add new content several times a week.

- **REPAIR BROKEN LINKS.** It's a fact of the Webmaster's life: links to external sites go bad. Rather than let one of my visitors get an "Error 404" message from a link on my site, I check and repair (or remove) links once every month or so.

- **TWEAK APPEARANCE, ORGANIZATION, AND NAVIGATION.** If you (or your Webmaster) are truly dedicated to the health and well-being of your Web site, you'll constantly be looking for ways to make it better, faster, more logically organized, and easier to navigate. Then you'll put your plans into action by tweaking pages as necessary to make them better.

Of course, if your Web site is nothing more than an online brochure or catalog, you probably won't have much to maintain. But I hope your site will be more than that. It can be.

## Additional Fees & Hidden Costs

You may run into other fees and costs not specifically covered in this chapter. That's because some Web consultants and ISPs break down their fees, separating items that are often "included" in fees charged by other Web consultants or ISPs. Or perhaps the Web consultant or ISP can't provide a specific service and you need to hire someone else to provide it.

For example, The Chicago Safe Company Web site (see Figure 3.1) may have been expensive (by my standards, anyway), but you have to admit that the graphics look good. Fortunately, the cost of preparing them was included in the price tag. But some Web developers don't have the skills necessary to create good graphics. If they can't do the job, someone else has to. And that's where additional fees may arise.

Just as some people can't draw, others can't write. That's where professional writers, stepping in as content authors, can help. They can take the most ho-hum business and write a description about it that makes it sound great. But be prepared to pay for this service if it isn't something your Web designer provides.

## Food for Thought

Now that you have some idea of what it may cost to build your Web presence, take a moment to think about the costs and how you can minimize them. Use these questions to get started. If you'd like to share your thoughts with other readers or see what other readers have to say, visit the book's companion Web site, http://www.smallbusinessonweb.com/.

○ Based on the list of skills and knowledge required to design and build a Web site, do you have what it takes? Could you be your company's Web designer?

○ If you or another company employee were busy building a Web site instead of doing your usual job, what would the impact on your company be?

○ Go back to your answers to the questions at the end of Chapter 2 and think about the kind of Web site you want to build. Who do you think would be the best and most cost-effective choice for designing, building, and maintaining that site for you: you, an in-house Web designer, or a Web consultant? And why?

○ In your situation, do you think it's worth the extra cost to have your own domain name? Why?

# CHAPTER FOUR

# Web Hosting Options

Chapter 3 briefly discusses Web hosting—
publishing your site's pages on a Web server so
they can be accessed by the world. There are
many Web hosting options, each of which has its
own pros, cons, and costs. This chapter explores
all options to help you decide which ones best
meet your needs without breaking your budget.

## In This Chapter

ISP Web Hosting

Server Co-Location

On-Premises Server

# ISP Web Hosting

At the bottom of the Web hosting options ladder is ISP Web hosting. In this method of hosting your Web site, all of your site's pages reside on your ISP's server, along with the Web sites of other businesses and individuals.

## Two Methodologies

As discussed in Chapter 3, most ISPs offer two ways for you to use their servers to host your Web site:

○ Set up your Web site as a subsite of the ISP's main site.

○ Set up your Web site as a **VIRTUAL DOMAIN** on the ISP's server.

## Being a Subsite

Being a subsite of your ISP's Web site is the least expensive Web serving option and almost every ISP offers it. Even AOL offers members the ability to create Web sites on the AOL server. (Visit http://hometown.aol.com/ to explore some AOL member pages; see Figure 4.1.)

Here's how it works. The ISP sets up a folder on its server in which your Web site's files—Web pages, images, etc.—will be stored. For addressing purposes, your Web site's URL is the name of the ISP's Web server, followed by a slash and the name of your folder, like this: http://www.wickenburg-az.com/ranchdressings/. (On UNIX-based servers, you may also have to include a tilde character before the folder name, like this: http://www.wickenburg-az.com/~ranchdressings/.) When a visitor types that URL into his Web browser, the default Web page for that folder (normally named *index.htm*, *index.html*, *default.htm*, or *default.html*) is displayed.

Your folder is secured from unauthorized uploads (or changes) by a user ID and password. To add or change content on your site, you upload new or revised files to your folder via FTP. (I tell you more about that in Chapter 10.)

**FIGURE 4.1**
The AOL Hometown page offers tools for building and searching AOL Web pages, as well as links for exploring existing pages.

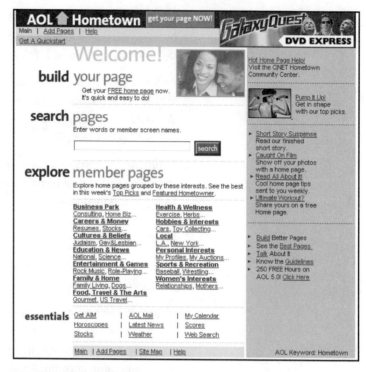

## Virtual Domain Hosting

Virtual domain hosting enables you to have your own domain name without the bother (or cost) of maintaining a Web server and direct Internet connection. To site visitors, it appears that you have your own Web server.

The ISP's job for setting up a virtual domain is a bit more complex than setting up for a subsite. The ISP still sets up a folder for your site's contents on its Web server. But it also sets up domain mapping information so your domain name will be associated with your folder on the server. Meanwhile, your domain name must be properly associated with your ISP's server in the domain name system—something you do when you set up a domain name, as discussed in Chapter 3. Then,

**VIRTUAL DOMAIN HOSTING**
A Web serving method in which your Web site is served from your ISP's server using your domain name.

when a site visitor enters a URL with your domain name, such as http://www.chromecaballeros.com/, the Web server displays the default document in your folder.

As far as you're concerned, maintaining your Web site as a virtual domain works the same way as if your site was a subsite. You upload files to your password-protected folder to add or change site content.

Additional benefits that come with virtual hosting often include the ability to use your own CGIs and one or more e-mail addresses using your domain name.

### What It Costs

Costs vary from one ISP to another. I've seen prices ranging from free to $60 per month or more, depending on the service you need.

If all you're interested in is setting up your Web site as a subsite on your ISP's server, the cost is probably already included in the cost of your dialup connection to the ISP. That means it's free with your dialup account. Be sure to check with your ISP for limitations, including site size and throughput limitations.

If you're interested in virtual domain hosting, expect to pay a setup fee of $0 to $150 (plus the domain name registration fee I told you about in Chapter 3), followed by monthly hosting fees of $15 to $60. One ISP I stumbled across while researching this book, Virtual Avenue (http://www.virtualave.net/) offers free virtual domain hosting. The catch? You have to display an advertisement on each of your Web pages.

### Pros & Cons

Why consider ISP Web hosting? Here are some of the benefits:

○  ISP Web hosting is the least expensive way to put a Web site online.

○  Your Web site will have a high-speed connection to the Internet. The actual connection speed varies by ISP.

- Your Web site will be backed up and protected against power failures and similar problems along with the rest of the ISP's system. All reputable ISPs have some kind of backup strategy.

Sounds great, doesn't it? But there are some limitations to consider:

- Some ISPs limit the amount of disk space your site can use or charge additional fees if you use more disk space than offered. Most ISPs offer from 5 MB to 20 MB of disk space; this is usually enough for most small business sites.

- Some ISPs limit or prevent the use of **CGIs**. This could prevent you from including features on your Web site such as counters, e-mail and other forms, or message boards.

- Many ISPs do not provide access to Web usage logs that track visitors to your site. As a result, you can't really get an idea of how many hits each page on your site gets.

- Some ISPs charge an additional fee if your site uses more than a preset maximum **BANDWIDTH**. This means that the more popular your site is, the more it will cost you to maintain.

**TIP ▶** *I discuss the pros and cons related to URLs, branding, and portability for each ISP hosting methods back in Chapter 3. Be sure to read that discussion before deciding which method is right for you.*

---

*For most small businesses, virtual domain hosting is an excellent way to get a Web site online quickly, easily, and cost effectively.*

---

**CGI (COMMON GATEWAY INTERFACE)**
A small program that performs a specific task on a Web server, such as processing a form or displaying a hit counter.

**BANDWIDTH**
The amount of information that passes through a network connection. The more information your Web site displays, the higher the bandwidth it uses.

## Finding an ISP

It's a fact of life: the only way to access the Internet is via an ISP. If you don't have an ISP and want to access the Internet, you'll have to get one.

If you don't have any way to access the Internet, you can start looking for an ISP with your local phone book or newspaper and a telephone. Telephone companies often offer ISP services, too; call the customer service department for your phone company to find out if Internet service is available in your area.

If you have access to the Internet at work or a friend's house, you can check The List (http://www.thelist.com/; see Figure 4.2), a Web site that provides a searchable list of ISPs in the United States and Canada. The List has been around a long time—I remember using it to find my first ISP back in 1994—and it has thousands of entries.

When choosing an ISP, make sure it offers a local phone number, high-speed access (at least 56 kbps), and free technical support. For more tips for choosing an ISP, check the August 1997 issue of *Macintosh Tips & Tricks*, which includes an article titled "Three Cs: Tips for Choosing an Internet Service Provider" by Patricia Delich, MA. You can find it in PDF format on the companion Web site for this book, http://www.smallbusinessonweb.com/.

FIGURE 4.2
The List is a great place to start your search for a new ISP.

## Server Co-Location

The next step up on the Web hosting options ladder is something called server co-location. This usually offers more flexibility than publishing on your ISP's server, but it's also more expensive.

## How It Works

Server co-location works one of two ways: either you put your own Web server at an ISP's facility or the ISP sets up a Web server for you at its facility. In either case, a Web server is dedicated to your Web site and it's connected to the Internet via high-speed Internet connection.

Your responsibilities vary depending on whether you have your own Webmaster to set up and maintain the site or you are depending on the ISP to do the job for you. As you can imagine, the more the ISP does for you, the more it will cost and the less control you will have over your site's maintenance. But if you lack the expertise to set up and manage a Web site, this can be a blessing.

You may also be required to provide the hardware (computer, router, cables, etc.) and software (Web server software, e-mail software, FTP software, etc.) for the Web server. If the ISP provides this, it will charge you accordingly.

Because the Web server is not in your location, you'll still use FTP to upload Web site files to your server. Site visitors will access your site by entering your site's domain name, such as http://www.wickenburg-az.com/.

## What It Costs

A small percentage of ISPs offer server co-location options. The fees vary widely by ISP, so be sure to ask about all fees when comparison shopping.

Table 4.1 summarizes the setup and monthly fees I found for this service:

TABLE 4.1 SERVER CO-LOCATION FEES

| SERVICE | SETUP FEE | MONTHLY FEE |
| --- | --- | --- |
| ISP-provided server | $500–$1,500 | $400–$800 |
| Client-provided server | $100–$500 | $250–$500 |

## Pros & Cons

There are three main benefits to using server co-location:

o   Your Web site is served from its own dedicated Web server. This
    means that all of the computer's resources can be used to serve
    your Web site's content rather than shared by multiple Web sites or
    other functions.

o   You should be able to put any software you like on the Web server.
    This enables you run whatever CGIs, Web log analysis software, or
    other programs you want to run in conjunction with your Web site.
    (I tell you more about Web server logs and log analysis software in
    Chapter 12.)

o   Because your Web site is at your ISP's location, it gets the benefit
    of your ISP's high-speed access to the Internet.

There are a few drawbacks, though:

o   Some ISPs base their monthly fees on bandwidth usage. That
    means that the more popular your Web site is, the more it will cost
    to serve.

o   Server co-location isn't cheap. (But it can be less expensive than
    having an on-premises server.)

o   You may be responsible for all server maintenance, including
    backups, software upgrades, and new software installations. That
    means you'll have to have the expertise (or hire someone with the
    expertise) to perform technical tasks reliably.

o   Because the server is not on your premises, you have to hope that
    the ISP can handle power outages, power surges, and other
    occurrences that may interrupt service to your site's visitors.

# On-Premises Server

At the very top of the Web hosting ladder is having your own on-premises Web server. Ah, what a luxury—and what a responsibility—*and* what an expense!

## How It Works

An on-premises Web server is just that—a Web server that resides on your premises. Your Webmaster sets up the hardware, installs the software, and connects the whole thing to a direct Internet connection. He then configures the whole thing with your domain name information, installs the Web page files, and opens it up to the world.

## What You Need

There are three basic ingredients to a Web server: hardware, software, and an Internet connection. Here's a closer look at each.

**TIP ▶** *Netopia, Inc., a company that sells Internet equipment, has an excellent FAQ page with questions and answers about connecting to the Internet. Look for it at http://www.netopia.com/equipment/tech/internetfaq.html.*

## Hardware

Start with a computer. The computer you select must be capable of running the Web server software and any other software required to run and maintain your Web site. It must also have enough disk storage space to hold all of the site's program and document files. For a small site—like the one most small businesses would need—you can often get away with a computer that's a year or two old. But for a larger site running powerful software, you may need a brand new machine.

**TIP ▶**  *Consult the system requirements section of your software documentation* before *buying a new machine for a Web server.*

You'll also need hardware to connect the computer to the Internet, such as a **MODEM** or **ROUTER**. The type of device you need varies depending on your Internet connection method. If you use a router, you'll also need the ingredients for a **LAN**, including Ethernet cards, hubs, and cables.

## Software

Like any other computer, your Web server computer needs software to run. Here's a quick rundown of the kind of software you may need:

○ **OPERATING SYSTEM SOFTWARE.** This varies based on your computer. For Intel machines, your choices are Windows 95/98/2000, Windows NT, Novell Netware, or some form of Unix. For Macintosh, your choices are Mac OS or Mac OS Server.

○ **NETWORKING SOFTWARE.** If your system is part of a network, you must install and configure the appropriate networking software.

○ **IP SOFTWARE.** Internet protocol software enables your computer system to exchange information with the Internet. Normally, this will be part of your operating system or networking software.

○ **DOMAIN NAME SYSTEM SERVER SOFTWARE.** DNS server software enables your computer to communicate with the domain name system so your domain name can be found. This software may not be required if your ISP allows you to use its DNS server for lookups; most do.

○ **WEB SERVER SOFTWARE.** This is the software that enables you to serve Web pages. Many options are available, from basic shareware packages to complete Internet server solutions.

- ○ **FTP SERVER SOFTWARE.** This software is necessary if you plan to use FTP to upload updated Web page files. It also enables you to offer FTP file downloads to site visitors.

- ○ **E-MAIL SERVER SOFTWARE.** This software is necessary if you plan to set up e-mail accounts on the server.

- ○ **LOG ANALYSIS SOFTWARE.** If you plan to keep track of page hits, referrers, and other usage statistics, you'll need software to take the raw log data and turn it into something you can make sense of.

- ○ **OTHER UTILITY SOFTWARE.** You'll probably want to back up your Web server on a regular basis and occasionally examine it for viruses and directory corruption. You'll need software do to it right.

**TIP ▶** *Want to research Web server software options before you make a purchase decision? Visit ServerWatch on Internet.com, http://serverwatch.internet.com/. This site is jam-packed with information about all kinds of servers, including feature comparisons, demo and update downloads, and links to server developer Web sites.*

### Internet Connection

To serve Web pages, you need a 24/7 connection to the Internet. Several options are available to small businesses:

- ○ **DIALUP** connections use standard telephone lines with modems to provide Internet access at speeds from 28.8 Kbps (or slower, but let's not even think about that!) to 168 Kbps. For higher speeds, special dual analog modems are required.

**MODEM**
A hardware device that enables a computer to exchange data over telephone lines. A modem is required for dialup connections to the Internet.

**ROUTER**
A hardware device that enables computers on a LAN to share a single Internet connection.

**LAN (LOCAL AREA NETWORK)**
A network of computers located in the same physical area—normally, within the same building.

- DDS (**DIGITAL DATA SERVICE**) or **LEASED LINE** connections use digital technology for 24/7 access to provide Internet access at speeds of 56 Kbps or 64 Kbps.

- DSL (**DIGITAL SUBSCRIBER LINE**) connections use standard telephone lines and DSL routers to provide Internet access at speeds from 144 Kbps to 1.54 Mbps. Types of DSL include SDSL, IDSL, ADSL, and UADSL.

- ISDN (**INTEGRATED SERVICES DIGITAL NETWORK**) is a digital telecommunications technology that simultaneously transmits voice and data over the same wires. For data connections such as Internet access, transfers at speeds up to 128 Kbps are possible. To use this technology, a special ISDN modem or router is required.

- T1 is a 24/7 direct connection to the Internet with speeds of up to 1.5 Mbps. A T1 connection can also be leased in "fractions" with access speeds of 56 Kbps per fraction.

Costs of each of these options vary widely from one ISP to another. They also vary by region. Generally speaking, the faster your connection, the more it'll cost you. Unless you already have the hardware required for one particular option, your best bet is to compare the costs of each appropriate option with each ISP you are considering before making a decision.

Your Internet connection must come with at least one **STATIC IP ADDRESS** (or one per computer and router if you have a LAN). This address is associated with your domain name in the domain name system.

### Webmaster or System Administrator

Once you have the computer, the software, and the Internet connection, you need someone with the know-how to put it all

**STATIC IP ADDRESS**
An IP address, assigned by your ISP, that is always the same. This IP address is associated with your domain name in the domain name system.

together and build a Web server that works. That's where the Webmaster or System Administrator comes in.

If your Web site is relatively small and basic, you can probably hire a Webmaster who can design and build your Web site, then set up and maintain your Web server. Chances are, this person will handle all your Web-related jobs but only those jobs. Managing a Web server and maintaining a Web site can be a full time job, even for small sites.

If your company has a network (or builds one in conjunction with the new Web server), a System Administrator can handle all of the network-related tasks, including setting up and maintaining the Web server. For small companies with small networks, this person might also handle some of the basic computer-related

## Serving It Yourself—On a Budget

I don't run a big company and I'm not independently wealthy. But I do have my own Web server right in my office. Here's how I did it without spending a fortune.

First, the hardware. Because of the work I do, I'm forced to upgrade my computer system once every 2 to 3 years. My old computers become "test mules" or find homes with relatives. But my old Power Macintosh 8500/180 became my Web server. With 96 Mbytes of RAM and a 2 Gbyte hard disk, it was all I needed. So I can argue that the computer was free; after all, it was fully depreciated.

Other hardware I needed included a router (about $700) and an Ethernet hub ($150). I already had the hub for my Ethernet network. The Power Macintosh has Ethernet networking built in, so no additional cards were required.

For operating system software, I stuck with Mac OS 9, which has support for Internet protocol and Ethernet networking. For Web serving software, I choose WebSTAR Server suite, which offers Web serving, FTP, and e-mail capabilities. Not only is this program popular among Macintosh Webmasters, but it is extremely easy to set up and use and is extensible through the use of plug-ins. The cost: $599.

For my Internet connection, I opted for an 24/7 ISDN connection at 128 Kbps and no limitation on bandwidth. The phone company set up a special phone line from Wickenburg to Phoenix that effectively gives me a Phoenix phone number. My ISP dials into my ISDN router which then talks to my Web server via the Ethernet hub. An added benefit to all this is that each of the computers on my network has its own IP address and can access the Web via direct connection. No more dialup service! The cost: $100 setup fee (to the phone company) plus $225 per month (to my ISP) and $75 per month (to the phone company). (ISDN costs vary based on location; chances are, it's cheaper where you live.)

The bottom line: my Web server cost approximately $1,550 to set up and costs $300 per month to maintain. With it comes a direct Internet connection for all my e-mail and Web surfing needs.

tasks, such as evaluating computer and software purchases, providing technical support, and configuring new computer systems brought into the company.

In every organization—even the smallest one—there's always one person who seems to "have a knack" for computer-related things. Think twice before giving this person the job of setting up and managing a Web server or network. It isn't easy and, if he screws things up, it can cost time and money to hire someone who does know what he's doing to fix the damage. It's better to get things off on the right track by hiring a knowledgeable person than to try to cut costs by having a novice do the job.

## What It Costs

This is the big question and I admit I don't have the answer. You'll have to figure it out for yourself based on the options you select for your hardware, software, Internet connection, and Webmaster or System Administrator.

A relatively generous budget might look something like this:

TABLE 4.2 IN-HOUSE SERVER BUDGET

| ITEM | POSSIBLE COST |
|------|--------------:|
| Computer | $ 3,000 |
| Modem or router with network components (if required) | $ 1,000 |
| Software | $ 3,000 |
| Internet connection setup | $ 500 |
| Total setup (one-time) costs | $ 7,500 |
| Internet connection monthly access | $ 500 |
| Webmaster or System Administrator Monthly Salary | $ 5,000 |
| Total monthly costs | $ 5,500 |

Remember, I did say "generous." You can do it for less. But you can also spend a heck of a lot more.

## Pros & Cons

Here are a few of the benefits to having your own Web server:

○ Your Web site is served from its own dedicated Web server, so all of the computer's resources can be used to serve your Web site's content.

○ You have complete control over your Web server, so you can install and use any software or utilities you like. This enables you to run whatever CGIs, Web log analysis software, or other programs you want to run in conjunction with your Web site.

○ You can set up your Web server to perform e-mail and FTP serving functions. This enables you to have in-house e-mail and file transfer features.

○ Your Web server can also act as an intranet server, serving secured internal files to the computers on your LAN. Keep in mind that there are special security issues and software that may be necessary to protect these documents from outsiders on the Internet.

○ If your Web server's Internet connection is handled through a router and LAN, that same connection is available to all computers on the network. This means individual computers will no longer need modems, dialup connections, and dedicated data phone lines to access the Internet.

And now for the bad news:

○ Having your own in-house Web server can be very expensive!

○ You must have an individual on staff who can maintain the system and troubleshoot problems.

○ You are responsible for backing up the system and providing power protection.

# Food for Thought

Ready to digest some of this information? Here are some questions to get you thinking. To see what other readers have come up with or share your thoughts, visit the book's companion Web site at **http://www.smallbusinessonweb.com/**.

○ Based on your budget and your plans for your Web site (as determined at the end of Chapters 2 and 3), which Web hosting option do you think is best for you? Why?

○ If you currently have an ISP, what do you like or dislike about it? If you don't have an ISP or are interested in switching to another one, what are the ISP services that are important to you?

# PART II

# Building Your Site

If you've read this far, you're already convinced that a Web site can benefit your business and it's within your budget. The next step is to design and build the site.

That's what this part of the book is all about. It tells you about the content and features you can include in your site, discusses design, and then helps you get started building the site yourself or provides helpful information for hiring and working with a Web designer. At the conclusion of this part's five chapters, your site will be ready to unveil to the world.

# Part II Table of Contents

# CHAPTER FIVE

# Site Content

A Web site's *content* is the information that is available on the site. Theoretically, it's the reason people visit a site—to get information they need about your business and its products or services. The more useful information visitors can get, the more likely they are to visit your site again.

This chapter lists and explains many of the content options you should consider as you decide what your site's pages should include. It also introduces the concept of content responsibility.

## In This Chapter

The Bare Minimum

Meeting Your Objectives

Content Responsibility

# The Bare Minimum

Let's start with the bare minimum: the information that should appear on every small business Web site. I'm hoping you already thought of these things.

## Business Name

This may sound like a real no-brainer, but it's important to provide the correct, complete name of your business on your Web site. You want to make sure that visitors know which business they're visiting online. This is especially important if you have competition with a similar sounding name or your Web site's URL does not accurately reflect your business name.

Here's an example. Coldwell Banker Bob Nuth & Associates (http://www.wickenburgrealestate.com/) is the local office of the nationwide real estate chain Coldwell Banker. When selecting a domain name for his site, owner Bob Nuth wanted a name that identified what his business does. He selected and registered the name wickenburgrealestate.com. Unfortunately, another real estate firm in town is called Wickenburg Property Management—a name that is similar to Bob's domain name. Bob prevents confusion between his firm and other local Realtors by clearly identifying his firm throughout his Web site, using Coldwell Banker logos and colors (see Figure 5.1).

### A Trend to Avoid: Trading Content for Pizzazz

I've been surfing the Web for years now and have seen Web pages progress from simple collections of detailed information to graphic-intensive, flashy, animated blobs of color. It seems that most Web designers are more interested in building a site that looks good than one that provides information that can be found, read, and understood.

Don't fall into this trap! Content should be your primary concern when deciding what should be included on your Web site. The more information you provide, the more your [potential] customers and clients can learn when they visit your site.

Remember Chapter 2? That's where I discussed what a Web site can do for you. Keep your objectives in mind throughout the Web site planning process.

## Business Description

Here's another no-brainer: providing a description of what your company does. This is especially important if the name of your business doesn't shed any light on the products or services you offer.

Chrome Caballeros Tours (http://www.chromecaballeros.com/) is a good example. The name tells you that it has something to do with tours, but the rest is a mystery—especially if you don't know what a *caballero* is. (It's Spanish for *knight*; does that help?) But owner Dave Waddell makes it clear what his company does right on his Web site's home page (see Figure 5.2), through the use of detailed descriptions and color photographs of his motorcycle camping adventures.

## Contact Information

Here's another basic piece of information that is sometimes missed: complete contact information. Some people (like me!) use the Web as a tool for looking up mailing addresses, phone numbers, or e-mail addresses for companies like yours.

FIGURE 5.1
The Web site for Coldwell Banker Bob Nuth & Associates clearly identifies the company, through the use of logos and colors.

**FIGURE 5.2**

The Chrome Caballeros Home page makes it clear what the company does, through the use of detailed descriptions and photographs.

*Chrome Caballeros*

*Roughin' It In Style*

**HOME**

**TOURS**

**DATES**

**SIGN UP**

**GALLERY**

**LINKS**

*Chrome Caballeros Tours*
1280 N. Vulture Mine Road
Wickenburg, AZ 85390

Toll Free (US): 877-684-5799
Outside US: 520-684-5799
Fax: 520-684-0486

E-Mail: ChromeCabDW@vr3az.net
Web: www.chromecaballeros.com

*Dear Friends,*

*Thank you for considering a Chrome Caballeros Adventure tour.*

*If you are really looking for a break from the norm, give us a call, you won't be disappointed.*

*I look forward to riding with you.*

*Sincerely,
Dave Waddell
President, Chrome Caballeros*

*Motorcycle Camping Adventures*

*Is your idea of a great motorcycle ride a winding two-lane road through majestic scenery; topped off with a hearty cowboy meal, cooked and served under the stars?*

**Then a *Chrome Caballeros* Tour is for you.**

We'll start with your steel horse on a two-lane blacktop through some of the most spectacular country in the world, throw in a tent and sleeping bag and top it off with some of the best cowboy camp meals you've ever tasted.

Best of all, it's all done for you. *Chrome Caballeros* takes care of everything, leaving you free to relax and enjoy three of the things you love most -- riding your bike, camping, and great food.

We furnish the camping gear and the food, and we transport your luggage, so you can bring what you need.

You'll spend your first night in the scenic high desert foothills of Wickenburg, Arizona, where the camp will be set up on a real working horse ranch. Like all our overnight camps, we'll be in an established campground with clean restroom facilities.

You'll be provided a tent big enough that you can actually stand up and put your pants on, a quality sleeping bag, even a pillow and a cot you can actually sleep on.

You'll meet the best camp cooks in the West. Jim and Roxie will cook up a gourmet cowboy dinner that will melt in your mouth. Then you'll be given a route map for the next day's ride and have an opportunity to get acquainted with your fellow caballeros.

You'll awaken from a good night's sleep to the smell of hot coffee and bacon frying.

After the best cowboy breakfast you've ever had, you'll pack your personal luggage, leave it in your tent, and head out for a fantastic day, riding at your own pace to the night's campsite.

Our routes are carefully planned along the most motorcycle-friendly roads in the west. A typical day's ride will cover approximately 200 miles, so you'll have plenty of time for sightseeing, exploring, and photography. In order to allow you the freedom to ride at your own pace, lunch is not included, but you're sure to find an irresistible little restaurant in one of the historic Old West towns on your route.

You'll arrive at the campground each evening to find camp all set up and dinner cookin'. Your luggage will be in your tent along with a fresh towel and washcloth so you can wash off the trail dust. Then you can relax by the fire and share the day's experiences with the rest of the caballeros till Jim rings the dinner bell.

After dinner, we might set up our new ETX-90 telescope for anyone who happens to be in the mood for stargazing. Or we might make a churn of ice cream. Then we'll give you your route map for the next day's ride.

All tours end back in Wickenburg, where we'll have a special farewell dinner for our last night together. Of course, we'll serve breakfast before you head home, loaded with enough photographs and memories to last until we meet again on another *Chrome Caballeros Tour* .

Contact information should include:

○ Company name and primary mailing address.

○ Mailing addresses of branch offices.

○ Phone and fax numbers for individuals or departments customers or clients may want to contact. Be sure to include a toll-free number if you have one.

○ E-mail addresses for individuals or departments customers or clients may want to contact.

It's also a good idea to indicate how long it might take for a customer or client to get a return phone call or e-mail message. For example, if you check e-mail once a day during the work week, you may want to warn site visitors that they should expect a response to e-mail inquiries within one business day.

### Hours of Operation

If your business keeps specific hours, be sure to tell site visitors what those hours are—including the time zone! This will prevent frustration among visitors who try to call you at 4 PM Pacific Time when your business is only open from 8 AM to 6 PM Eastern Time. It will also prevent site visitors from stopping by your place of business when you're closed.

# Meeting Your Objectives

When deciding on other information to include, remember your objectives for the Web site. What do you want it to do for you? That will determine what other information you should include.

Here are a few ideas to get you started.

*Your goal should be to make your Web site valuable enough to visitors that they want to bookmark it. Bookmarks are the best way to ensure repeat visits, but it's entirely up to the visitor to decide whether a site is worth bookmarking.*

### Product or Service Details

At the very minimum, you'll probably want to include a list of your products and services. But why not go into detail? Pull information from your brochures and catalogs. Then expand that information to bring it up to date or get more specific. Think of the questions your customers or clients might have and answer them in the descriptions.

### Pricing Information

By providing pricing information, you help your customers or clients do some comparison shopping. They can see at once if your prices are within their budgets. If you have some kind of special offer available to Web customers or clients, or special pricing for qualified wholesalers, don't keep it a secret. Provide as much information as you can.

Not everyone likes to include pricing information where it is publicly accessible to customers or clients—as well as the competition. Instead, some companies prefer to have a sales representative contact the customer or client directly. If this is the case in your business, be sure to explain on your site how customers or clients can get pricing information. Just be aware that a visit to your Web site might be the last step in a purchase decision—if the pricing information isn't readily available, the visitor could buy elsewhere.

### Support Information

If you have technical support documents, FAQs, and other documents that can help your current customers and clients, put them on your Web site. As discussed in Chapter 2, this can save you the trouble (and expense) of sending this information out by fax or mail. Best of all, you can make the information available to your customers or clients 24/7 so they can solve problems when they occur—not when you're around to help them.

### The Four "A"s

Another marketing tool is something I refer to as the Four "A"s.

The Four "A"s give potential customers or clients confidence in your company's capabilities. Just make sure that the item you include on your site is related to your company. Otherwise, it'll appear as if you're trying to impress potential customers or clients with irrelevant information.

### Affiliations

Affiliations are organizations with which your business or its principals are affiliated. If your business is part of a larger organization, be sure to say so on your Web site. It shows that you're not just some small fly-by-night company.

The same goes for professional and public service organization affiliations of the business owners or managers. It shows that these people take their profession and community seriously.

### Accreditations

Accreditations are certificates or degrees that the business or its principals have earned. These usually include completion of continuing education courses related to the business. Accreditations are extremely popular in professional services fields such as real estate, accounting, and finance. Certificates or degrees earned by business owners or managers show that these people are always interested in learning more about their profession so they can better serve their customers or clients.

### Accolades

Accolades are words of praise from customers or clients. They can be testimonials, letters of thanks, or just quotes about the company's capabilities. Accolades are a great way to show how real customers and clients feel about your company.

**TIP ▶** *Be sure to get permission from a customer or client to use his comments on your Web site before you put it online.*

**Web Site Design Awards**

A Web designer I know includes numerous award logos and graphics on many of the Web sites he creates. Most of these awards are from obscure sources and I suspect that he paid some kind of fee to obtain them. These awards say nothing about the content of the Web site or the quality of the company for which the site was built. They just make you wonder whether the Web designer spends more time building Web sites or entering design contests.

## Awards

Awards are just that: awards received by the business or its principals. They show that the business's service is good enough to be recognized by outside organizations.

## Staff Information

If your business provides a service to clients, you may want to include some information about the people who will be providing the service. Who are these people? How long have they been with the company? What are their accomplishments? Why should clients feel comfortable letting these people handle their needs? These are some of the questions the information you include could answer.

Again, the Coldwell Banker Bob Nuth & Associates Web site (http://www.wickenburgrealestate.com/) is a good example. It includes photos and bios of each real estate professional on its staff (see Figure 5.3). Potential clients can get to know the sales staff and choose the one that they think can meet their needs.

## Other Resources

If you know of other sources of information that could be of interest to customers or clients, include them on your Web site. This helps expand the information you provide without adding pages to the site.

For example, a tax accountant may provide information about where IRS forms and publications can be found in his area. Or he might list some Web sites with additional tax data. In both instances, he's helping the site visitor get more information, but he's not actually providing that information on his site.

**FIGURE 5.3**
Providing information about your sales or service staff can help site visitors select the right person to meet their needs.

## Site Revision Date

You may want to include the date your site (or individual pages on the site) was last revised. But beware! If your site isn't revised often, including the revision date will confirm what the visitor may already suspect: that the site's information is stale. In fact, some savvy Internet surfers (myself included) will look for a revision date to help ensure that the information isn't old. It may be better to leave the date out and keep them guessing.

On the other hand, if your site is updated on a regular basis—say, more often than once a month—it's a very good idea to include a revision date. This will assure visitors that your Web site's information is important enough to keep up to date and that the information there is fresh.

# Content Responsibility

A discussion of the site revision date is a perfect lead-in to the topic of content responsibility. You see, one of your responsibilities as a Web site owner is to keep the information on your site accurate and up to date. But that's not your only responsibility.

## Keep Information Current

The more detailed and time sensitive your site's information is, the more time and effort it will require to keep that information current. For example, The Chicago Safe Company's Web site (see Figure 3.1) is basically an online brochure. None of its information is time sensitive. As a result, it doesn't need to be updated very often at all.

But one of the Web sites I maintain, wickenburg-az.com (http://www.wickenburg-az.com/; see Figure 5.4) includes recent area news stories right on the Home page. If I don't update it at least once a week, the information will be stale and everyone will know it. The Web site will look poorly maintained in the eyes of site visitors.

Look at your site objectively, as if through the eyes of a site visitor seeing it for the first time. Then determine how often you need to update site pages to keep the content fresh.

**TIP ▶** *One way to encourage repeat visits to your site is to update site contents regularly. Add new, valuable information any time you can. Visitors who know about your site will keep coming back to see what's new. And if you're lucky, they'll tell their friends about your site, too.*

## Keep Information Accurate

Accuracy is extremely important on your Web site. Site visitors expect the information they find to be correct. Imagine the frustration (or even anger) when they discover that your product doesn't have all the features your site claims or it sells for a higher price than listed on your site.

Keeping information accurate shouldn't be that difficult. Simply review the site's contents regularly—especially right after you

**FIGURE 5.4**

The wickenburg-az.com Home page includes time sensitive information that must be updated regularly to stay fresh.

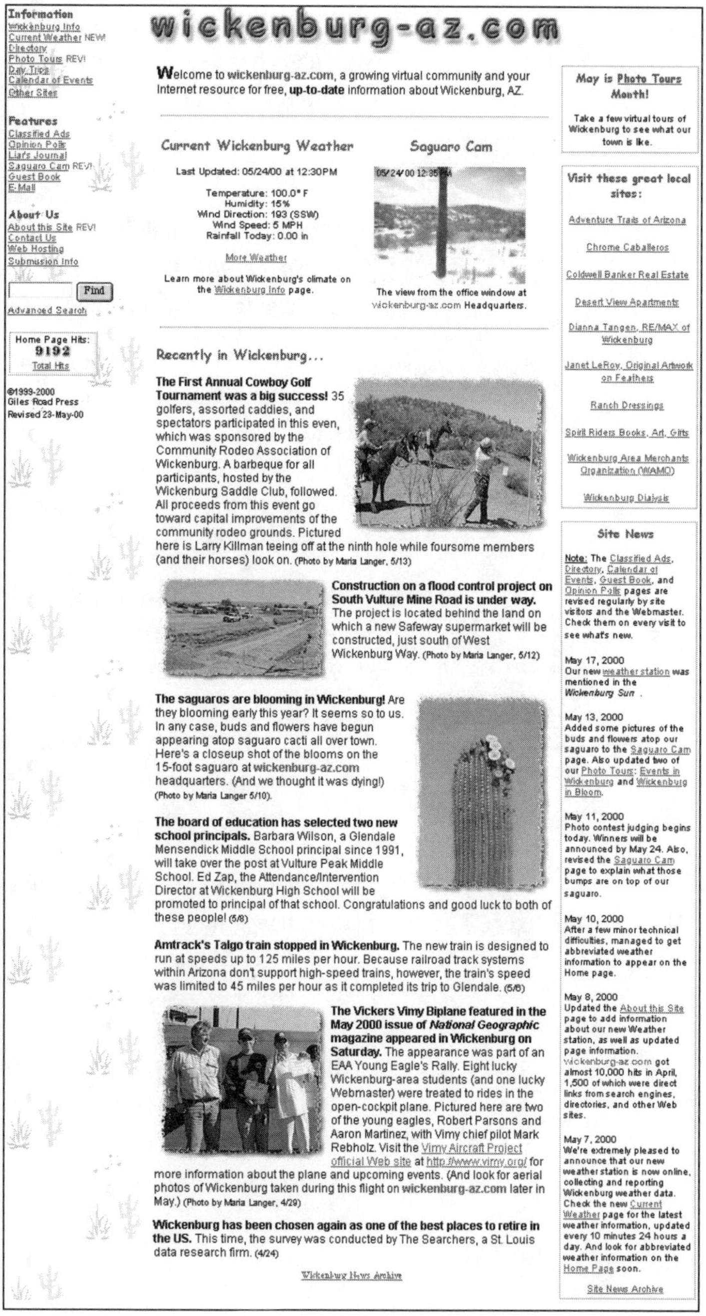

add or remove a product or service or make a price change. Make changes as necessary. Be thorough and don't let anything fall through the cracks.

## Respect Copyrights

On the Web, you'll find a lot of "borrowing"—using someone else's material in a Web site. Unfortunately, in many cases the borrowing is really copying and is against copyright law.

What does this mean to you as you gather content for your Web site? It means that you cannot simply take content—whether it's text, images, or sounds—from another source and include it on your Web site without the permission of the creator/copyright holder of that content. It doesn't matter if the source is in print or on the Web—if it isn't yours, it's protected by copyright law.

What if you find some great content that's just perfect for inclusion on your Web site? How do you include it without violating copyright law? I can think of two ways:

○ **GET THE WRITTEN PERMISSION OF THE COPYRIGHT HOLDER.** When requesting permission, you're likely to get one of three responses: no, yes, or yes if you pay a fee.

○ **INCLUDE A LINK TO THE CONTENT ON YOUR WEB SITE.** If the information is already on the Web, why reproduce it on your site? Simply describe the information on your site and include a link to it so visitors can see it where it legally resides.

Just remember that someone probably worked very hard to create that content. Reproducing it without permission is the same as stealing it. Not only is it dishonest and illegal, but it can get you and your company into trouble.

**TIP ▶** *Want to learn more about copyrights, especially as they relate to computer illustrations and Web publishing? Be sure to check out* **Electronic Highway Robbery,** *a Peachpit Press book by Mary E. Carter. You can learn more about it at http:// www.peachpit.com/books/catalog/88393.html. Or for a more general discussion of copyright information, visit the Library of Congress Copyright Office Web site at http:// www.loc.gov/copyright/.*

# Food for Thought

Now it's time to give this chapter some real thought. Here are a few suggestions to get the juices flowing. To share your thoughts with other site visitors or see what they had to say about this chapter's topics, be sure to visit the book's companion Web site at http://www.smallbusinessonweb.com/.

○ Make a list of the information you think you want to include on your site. Then number each item by importance, with #1 being the most important. Where do you think the top three items should appear on your site?

○ If you expect your site to be more than 3 pages, build an outline of the site's contents. Or chart the contents using an organization-chart format. Remember to build a logical flow of information; this can be used for the actual organization of your site.

○ Use your Web browser to visit at least ten Web sites for companies like yours. (Search engines or professional directories can help you find them.) Make a list of all the questions the site left unanswered. This is the content that was missing from the site.

# CHAPTER SIX

# Interface Elements & Features

A Web site's *interface elements* are the tools that the site visitor uses to access the site's content. Its *features* are specialized content that make the site more interesting. The proper use of interface elements and features can make a Web site more user friendly and interesting.

This chapter discusses the interface elements and features commonly found on Web sites so you can decide if they're right for yours.

## In This Chapter

BASIC ELEMENTS

FORM-BASED ELEMENTS & FEATURES

OTHER FEATURES

# Basic Elements

Most Web sites include three basic interface elements: format-ted text, hyperlinks, and graphics. Here's a closer look at each.

## Formatted Text

The most basic feature found on Web sites is formatted text.

Text is the most efficient way to present most kinds of informa-tion on a Web page—it loads quickly so it appears without delay in every visitor's browser window. Formatting enables you to make the text easier to read by including headings, bulleted or numbered points, indented quotes, and tables.

## Hyperlinks

One of the best features of the Web is the ability to link to other pages or other bits of information on the same page. Links make it easy and convenient for site visitors to find related informa-tion.

Links can be internal, external, or for e-mail. Here's the differ-ence between them and why you might want to include each type on your site.

### Internal Links

Internal links are links to related information on your Web site. These links, when used properly, improve site navigation while keeping visitors on your site.

Here's an example from the Coldwell Banker Bob Nuth & Associates site (http://www.wickenburgrealestate.com/). Each staff information page (see Figure 5.3) includes a link to the staff member's property listings. So when you read that Brenda specializes in "upper-end" properties, you can click her Property Listings link to view a list of some of the upper-end properties available in the area.

## Links to Other Web Sites

When the Web was in its infancy, it was a common practice to fill Web pages with links to other Web sites. The belief was that the people using the Web had nothing better to do than follow these links to learn more about a specific topic. Back in those days, there were far fewer sites to visit and, without good search engines to find information on the Web, these links were welcomed by Web surfers.

Nowadays, many small sites hesitate to include links to other sites, fearing that they'll lose site visitors who click these links. The truth of the matter is, the only thing keeping a visitor at your site is your site's content. If a visitor finds your site valuable, he'll stick around. If not, he'll go elsewhere, by clicking a link on your site or by using his Web browser's navigation features.

Dave Waddell, owner/operator of Chrome Caballeros (http://www.chromecaballeros.com/; see Figure 5.2) has no qualms about including links to quality sites on his site's link page. He's in the business of conducting motorcycle camping tours, but he's not in the business of providing motorcycles to the folks who use his service. So his Links page includes links to Phoenix-area companies that rent motorcycles. He does this as a service to his customers, helping them to find the right deal for motorcycle rentals.

*When you link to another Web site, you are, in effect, recommending that site to your site's visitors. Better make sure that every site you link to is one you'd want to recommend!*

**TIP ▶** *One way to handle links to external sites is to set up the link so that a new Web browser window opens with the linked page. This keeps your Web site's window open in the background. If you use this technique, use it sparingly because it tends to annoy some Web surfers.*

## Handling Requests for Reciprocating Links

If your site is good, chances are, other business owners or Webmasters will ask for a RECIPROCATING LINK. Don't link to another site unless that site meets these criteria:

○ The site should not be for a business that directly competes with yours. (Duh.)

○ The site must include content that is related to yours and is valuable to your site's visitors. Don't waste a customer or client's time with irrelevant information.

○ The site should meet your standards for design and appearance. Linking to an amateurishly prepared site can make your site (and your company) look bad.

○ If the site is for a business, that business should be managed with the same level of professionalism as yours. Linking to a fly-by-night operation can make you look bad, too.

The only way you can learn whether a site meets all of these criteria is to visit it and communicate with its owner, whether by e-mail or telephone.

### E-Mail Links

E-mail or "mailto" links make it easy for site visitors to send e-mail messages to an e-mail address you specify. The visitor clicks the link and his e-mail program automatically opens a new message window with the To field all filled out. The visitor simply enters his message and clicks the Send button to send it.

E-mail links are a convenience to site visitors. Any time you include an e-mail address on your Web site, you may want to turn that address into a mailto link to save visitors the bother of entering the address into an e-mail form.

**TIP ▶** *Do your visitors a favor: When setting up an e-mail link, be sure to clearly identify it as an e-mail link. Most Web surfers find it annoying to click a link that unexpectedly displays an e-mail form.*

### Graphics, Images, & Multimedia Elements

Graphics, images, and MULTIMEDIA elements perform two functions on Web sites:

- ○ **THEY MAKE THE SITE'S PAGES MORE INTERESTING**. These kinds of elements include buttons, rules, logos, icons, backgrounds, animations, movies, and sounds.

- ○ **THEY COMMUNICATE INFORMATION.** These kinds of elements include photographs or schematics of products, maps of your store or office locations, photographs of your facilities or staff, and interviews with customers or clients.

### What to Include

When deciding on graphics, images, and multimedia elements to include on your site, think about your reason for including them. If for appearance and interest only, be sure to read Chapter 7 for some important design considerations. If to communicate information, make sure you choose elements carefully so the most important information is what you share with site visitors.

### Formats & Plug-Ins

There are a few things to keep in mind when deciding on what kinds of graphics, images, and multimedia elements you should include in your site.

- ○ Not all of your Web site visitors will be able to see the graphics on your Web site. For example, some people keep images turned off in their Web browsers so pages load more quickly. Others may view your Web pages with hand-held Internet appliances, like PDAs and cell phones. For this reason, your site should not *depend* on graphics to communicate all of its content.

- ○ Many simple graphic elements can be created right within HTML. This includes horizontal rules and colors. Creating an element with

**RECIPROCATING LINK**
A link to another site in return for a link to your site on that site.

**MULTIMEDIA**
Any element that includes more than one method of communication.

HTML ensures that the element is properly supported by all Web browsers. A simple example is the companion Web site for one of my books, *FileMaker Pro 5 Companion* (**http://www.gilesrd.com/ fmprocomp/**). The site uses background colors within table cells to create simple graphic elements. The only "real" graphic on the Home page (see Figure 6.1) is the book cover.

o  All Web browsers support images in the following formats: GIF and JPEG. So, for maximum compatibility, you should probably stick to one of those formats. GIF is best for simple images with few colors (less than 216) while JPEG is best for photographs or more complex images with many colors. Some current browsers also support images in PNG format. All of these formats are cross-platform, so they can be viewed on any computer system that supports graphics.

o  Some multimedia formats require plug-ins to work. Some examples include QuickTime, Flash, Shockwave, and RealPlayer. If you include a multimedia element that requires a plug-in to work, you run the risk of your site's visitors not having the plug-in. The best you can do is provide a link to the plug-in on the page where

**FIGURE 6.1**
The companion Web site for *FileMaker Pro 5 Companion* makes extensive use of HTML for quick-loading, simple visual appeal.

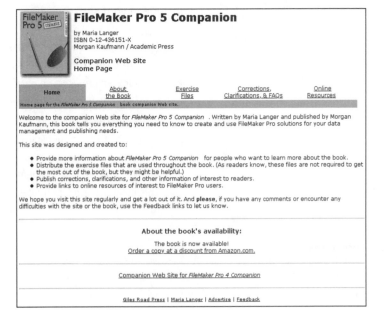

it's required, along with an explanation of what the element they're missing is all about. Just don't fool yourself into thinking that a visitor will download a plug-in just to see your Web page.

*Never include an interface element or feature that requires a specific browser or computer platform to function properly. Doing so tells site visitors that you don't care what browser or computer they use; they must use your choice to get full access to your site. Not very considerate, is it?*

# Form-Based Elements & Features

Forms add an element of interactivity to your Web site. The visitor enters information in one or more boxes or selects options, then clicks a button to make something happen.

**TIP ▶** *Forms work with CGIs, which determine what the form does. Your Web server must support the CGI you want to use for you to include the form-based feature on your Web site.*

Here are a few examples of how forms can be used on Web sites.

### E-Mail Forms

An e-mail form gathers information from site visitors, then sends that information to a specific e-mail address. For example, Chrome Caballeros (**http://www.chromecaballeros.com/**) uses a very simple e-mail form to generate leads for its tour business (see Figure 6.2).

### Database Interactivity

Forms can enable site visitors to access information stored in a database. Depending on how you set up the database interactivity, visitors can search and view database contents or add or modify database information.

For example, Coldwell Banker Bob Nuth & Associates (**http://www.wickenburgrealestate.com/**) maintains a database of property listings that it can update at any time. Site visitors can access the database by clicking links with predefined search criteria or by entering information in a search form. The results appear in a list with some basic information (see Figure 6.3); the

FIGURE 6.2
This simple form e-mails contact information and comments to the Chrome Caballeros staff from prospective customers.

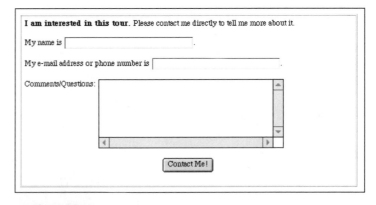

FIGURE 6.3
The Coldwell Banker Bob Nuth & Associates Web site features a searchable database of property listings.

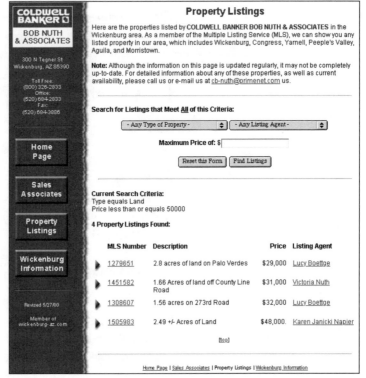

site visitor clicks an item to see its detail on another page (see Figure 2.1).

## Search Capabilities

If your site has more than a handful of pages, you should consider including a search feature. This makes it possible for site visitors to search for and find specific information on your site.

Search features work by combining a search CGI with an indexing program. Both run on the Web server. For example, on my server, I set up the WebSTAR Search Indexer program to automatically index the contents of one of my Web sites, wickenburg-az.com (http://www.wickenburg-az.com) every night. The program creates a database and the search CGI searches that for matches. It then displays a list of pages that match the search criteria (see Figure 6.4).

Not all ISPs support the ability to include search features on Web sites. Some who do support it may charge an additional fee to implement it. Ask your ISP or Webmaster if you can include this feature on your site.

TIP ▶ *If you can't include a search feature on your Web site, consider creating an index or contents page that lists and describes all pages on your site, with links to each page.*

## Guest Book

A guest book enables site visitors to share their thoughts and opinions about the site with other visitors. It's a great way to learn what visitors think—and make sure other visitors learn it, too.

Beware! Guest books can work for you or against you. If someone doesn't like you, your company, or your Web site, they can say negative things in your guest book for the world to see!

**FIGURE 6.4**

A tiny search form appears in the navigation bar on the left side of each page on wickenburg-az.com. Using the form displays a Search Results page like this one.

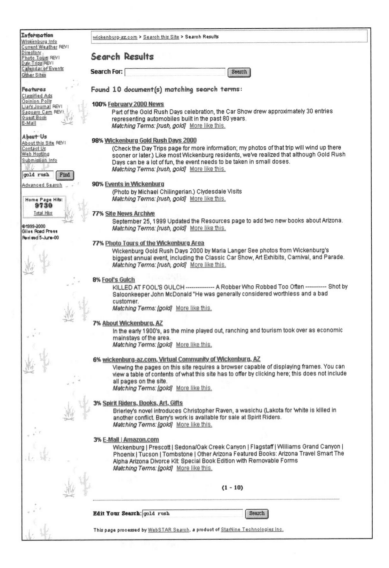

## FileMaker Pro

FileMaker Pro is an excellent tool for putting database information on the Web. I use it on my Web sites for feedback forms, guest books, classified ads, real estate listings, calendars, and opinion polls. One of my more creative applications is an articles database on the Vimy Aircraft Project Official Web Site (http://www.vimy.org/). Project volunteers can add articles to the database from anywhere in the world. The five most recent articles automatically appear on the site's Home page (see Figure 6.5). This keeps the site up-to-date with the minimum amount of effort on my part.

You can get more information about FileMaker Pro at http://www.filemaker.com/.

FIGURE 6.5

As shown in this example, a database doesn't have to *look* like a database. The five news stories in the "What's Happening" section of the Vimy Aircraft Project Home page are the last five entries in a database.

## VIMY AIRCRAFT PROJECT

Home

**The Silver Queen**
Some History
Building the Vimy
The Check Flight

**The Flights**
England to Australia
London to Cape Town
Articles

**Educational Project**
The Field Team
The Curriculum
Articles
Learn More

**News & Events**
Upcoming Events
Article Archive
Search for Articles

**Contact!**
Who's Who
Other Volunteers
The Sponsors
Becoming a Sponsor
Press Contacts
Vimy Discussion List
Guest Book
Past Correspondence

**Silver Queen Shop**

*" The Vimy is more than a flying machine made out of fabric, wood and wires – she is a vivid reminder to an often timid society that great adventure has always been the path of progress."*
- Peter McMillan, Owner/Pilot

Hits to this Page:
5 5 3 8

Site Revised 29-April-00

**Welcome to the Official Web Site for the Vimy Aircraft Project!**

This Web site provides information about the **Silver Queen** Vickers Vimy, its flights, and the educational project that was conducted during the 1999 London to Cape Town flight.

This is also where you can find up-to-date information about upcoming appearances of the Vimy at airshows throughout North America; articles about past appearances, flights, and educational project; and links to the Silver Queen Shop and sponsor sites.

The Vimy in flight.

### What's Happening

**5/8/2000: Vimy Featured in May 2000 Sport Aviation Magazine**

The Vimy is featured as the cover story in the May 2000 issue of Sport Aviation Magazine, the magazine of the EAA. The article, which has plenty of photographs, was written by Peter McMillan, John LaNoue, and Mark Rebholz. It provides a wealth of information about the Vimy, including how it was built and details of its two trip recreations to date.

The Vimy has special significance to EAA members as the largest homebuilt aircraft in the world. For more information about the EAA, visit its Web site.

**4/19/2000: Vimy News Now Appears on Home Page**

I've modified the Vimy Web Site so the latest five news stories always appear on the site's Home Page. This makes it really easy to see what's new with the Vimy Aircraft Project.

Older news stories can still be found with News area links, as well as the Search for Articles link.

As usual, I'm always interested in hearing feedback from site visitors about the site's appearance and functionality. I'll listen to suggestions, too! E-mail me at webmaster@gilesrd.com.

**4/3/2000: Vimy Featured in "Sport Aviation" Hot Line Piece**

The Vimy was mentioned in a 1/3 page article on page 13 of EAA's April 2000 "Sport Aviation" magazine. The article, which included a photo by Patty Rebholz (pilot Mark Rebholz's wife), mentioned the upcoming "National Geographic" article (look for it in the May 2000 issue) . The Web site was also mentioned.

**3/23/2000: Discussion List Added to Vimy Web Site**

To add an element of interactive communication to the Web site, we've added a public discussion list. The Vimy Aircraft Project Discussion List will allow subscribers to discuss Vimy-related news and events, as well as automatically send news reports (like this one) to list subscribers.

The list is moderated, so only those messages appropriate to the list will be passed on to subscribers. We expect it to generate approximately 10 messages per month.

You can learn more about the Vimy Discussion List and subscribe to it by following the Vimy Discussion Link in the NavBar of the Vimy Aircraft Project Official Web Site, http://www.vimy.org/.

**3/5/2000: USAIG Returns as a Major Sponsor**

USAIG has returned to the Vimy Project team as a major sponsor and will supply our insurance needs for our upcoming flying season. This is great news for our project because now we can confidently plan our appearances knowing we will be insured and able to participate in all events that require proper insurance, such as the EAA Young Eagles event scheduled for April 29 at the Wickenburg, Arizona airport. USAIG was our insurance sponsor for the VIMY 1994 flight from England to Australia and we are very happy to have them back with us. Many thanks to Patrick Healy and Peter McMillan for their efforts in securing this sponsorship that is so vital to the continued operation of the Silver Queen.

Last week the BOSE CORPORATION was sent a demo video and some sample slides from the England - Cape Town flight, all supplied by our project photojournalist Peter McBride. Dick Merriott, from BOSE, was very impressed with the images and is now organizing the display event for AirVenture 2000 (Oshkosh) that will focus on "The Flight of the Silver Queen" as the promotional display for this years event. BOSE will have a theatre at convention where the public can view many of the scenes from Africa while highlighting the performance of the BOSE headsets and flying helmets we used on the trip. I am sure this will be a very exciting display.

The month of May will be very exciting for us...look for the National Geographic article "Queen of the African Sky", and also the first in a series of articles in Sport Aviation, the journal of the Experimental Aircraft Association.

View all Articles | Search for Articles

### Our Sponsors

Another problem that sometimes occurs with guest books is people using a guest book to ask questions about your company, its products, or its services. You can limit the chances of this happening by clearly stating how the guest book should be used. For example, on wickenburg-az.com (http://www.wickenburg-az.com/) the Guest Book New Entry Form page (see Figure 6.6) warns visitors not to use the guest book to ask questions.

**TIP ▶**  *If you do include a guest book feature on your site, make sure you review all entries when they're entered. I set up my guest books so they automatically send a copy of new entries to me in e-mail messages. If an entry is unsuitable for the site, I know about it quickly and can remove it.*

Keep in mind that not all site visitors are interested in entering their comments in a guest book. Many believe that doing so will add them to some kind of junk e-mail list. If you do plan to use entry information for a mailing list, be sure to inform visitors.

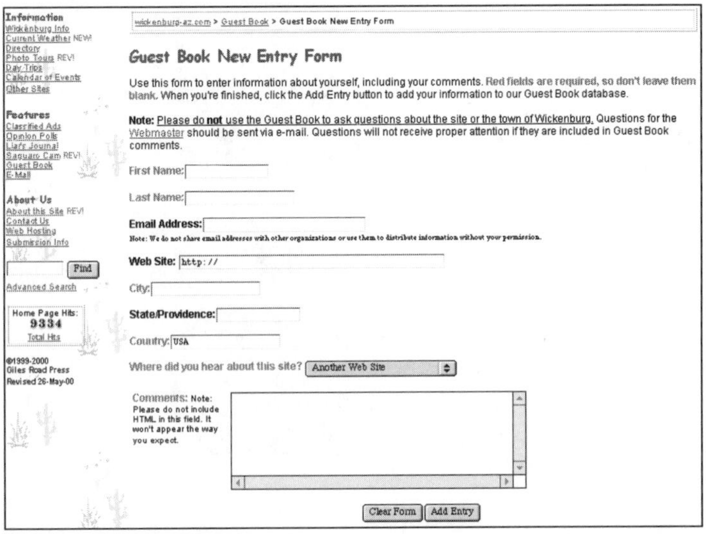

**FIGURE 6.6**
The Guest Book New Entry Form page on wickenburg-az.com includes the usual guest book fields, along with specific instructions.

# Other Features

Hit counters and online chat are two other features that are commonly found on Web sites. Here's why you might want to include—or avoid—these two features, as well as quick discussion about how you can learn about other features available for your site.

### Hit Counters

Counters keep track of the number of hits to a Web page. They are extremely popular with small business sites, primarily because site owners or Webmasters want a way to show how popular a site is.

Counters might be a good way to publicly show how many hits a site gets, but they're a terrible way to accurately monitor site usage. For example, if you put a counter on your Home page, all it tracks is hits to that page—not to the other pages of your Web site. With the ever-increasing usability of search engines, however, many of your site's visitors never even see your Home page—they go right to the page the search engine indicated.

Recently, a "rival" Web consultant used my Home page counter as evidence that his Web site was more popular than mine. (Yes, some people never do grow up.) The counter showed only several thousand hits for a one-month period when, in fact, the site had over 13,000 hits for the same period. Obviously, Home page hits aren't the same as site hits and not everyone visits the Home page.

**TIP ▶** *A better way to monitor site activity is with the logs created by your Web server software. Log analysis tools can make sense of the entries by summarizing hits and other data. I discuss log analysis software in Chapter 12.*

Another drawback to page counters is the number that appears. A friend of mine who hosts a site on my Web server added a counter to his site's sole page six months ago. I peeked at the page last week and saw that the counter read 17. Now *that* has to be depressing. And it sure makes the site look unpopular to the other sixteen people who looked at it. Sure, you can pad the number or have it count by twos or threes or tens, but that kind of defeats the purpose of a counter, doesn't it?

## Online Chat

If you're interested in building a community on your Web site, online chat is the way to go. This feature enables site visitors to type messages to each other in real time.

There are two potential problems with adding an online chat feature to a small business Web site:

- IN MOST CASES, THE CHAT FEATURE WON'T ADD ANYTHING OF VALUE FOR YOUR CUSTOMERS OR CLIENTS. Chances are, it'll just attract people who like to chat. Your resources could probably be better used on features that promote your business rather than entertain your site visitors.

- A CHAT FEATURE ISN'T VERY INTERESTING WHEN THERE AREN'T ANY CHATTERS. If your site gets a few hundred hits a day, how many of those people will wander into the chat area? How many of those people will enter a message to initiate a chat? And how many other people will be waiting around the chat area to participate?

Don't get the idea that I'm anti-chat. I'm not. But I am against including a chat feature simply because it's a cool thing to include.

Instead, consider using the chat feature for customer support. For example, establish regular chat hours where one of your company's representatives can be on hand to field questions and comments about your products or services. Or set up special event chats with knowledgeable people in your area of business. Make sure site visitors know when the chats will be held. Then cross your fingers and see who attends.

**TIP ▶** *If you'd like to see a great implementation of online chat, visit World Without Borders (http:// www.worldwithoutborders.com/). These folks know how to make a chat worth attending.*

## But Wait...There's More!

So far, I've covered the most popular Web site interface elements features. But there are more.

Get out your Web browser and go surfing to see what's included on other sites you admire. While you're at it, be sure to check out your competition's sites. Seeing what other folks have done with their sites is a good way to get ideas for what you want to include—or avoid—on your site.

# Food for Thought

Take a few moments to think about some of the interface elements and features covered in this chapter. Here are some suggestions. To share your thoughts with other readers or see what they had to say about this chapter's topics, visit the book's companion Web site at http://www.smallbusinessonweb.com/.

○ Which of the interface elements and features discussed in this chapter do you expect to include on your site? Why?

○ For each interface element or feature you plan to include on your site, list at least three ways you expect it to make the site better.

○ Use your Web browser to visit at least ten Web sites for companies like yours. (Search engines or professional directories can help you find them.) Make a list of the things you like and don't like about each site. Be objective!

# CHAPTER SEVEN

# Site & Page Design

Once you know what you want to include on your Web site and what tools site visitors will use to access it, you need to come up with an overall design for the site. This chapter tells you all about design considerations, from general appearance options to navigation. It also explains how and why you should work within the limitations of HTML.

## In This Chapter

DEVELOPING THE RIGHT LOOK

EFFECTIVE NAVIGATION

# Developing the Right Look

Your Web site is a virtual version of your store or office. The way your workplace looks has a direct impact on how customers or clients feel about you. The same goes for your Web site.

Here are some things to consider when developing the right look for your Web site.

**TIP ▶** *I could write an entire book about Web design, but I won't. Other authors have already done the job. My favorite—a book I highly recommend to people designing their first Web site— is* **The Non-Designer's Web Book,** *a Peachpit Press book by Robin Williams and John Tollett. Robin and John explain the elements of Web design in plain English. Their book is informative and fun to read. (And they got to do their pictures in color.) Learn more about the book at http://www.peachpit.com/books/catalog/68859.html.*

## First Impressions Count

Here's a scenario for you.

Say you need some legal advice and a friend has recommended a lawyer. When you arrive for your appointment, you discover that the lawyer's office is in a storefront on the bad side of town. In the reception area, the carpet is worn and dirty and paint is peeling off the walls. The receptionist's desk is missing a leg, so a whole corner of it is being propped up with fat law books that look like they were used for a cat's scratching post after they'd been in a flood. The receptionist, who is chewing a huge wad of gum, tells you to wait on one of the folding chairs set up against a wall. All the magazines on the TV table beside it have their covers torn off. What are you going to think about that lawyer?

Your Home page is like your store's entrance or your office's reception area. It's what people first see when they visit. Don't you think it's important to give visitors the right first impression?

## The Limitations of HTML

As you'll learn in Chapter 8, most Web pages are created with HTML, a MARKUP LANGUAGE that, when interpreted by a Web browser, displays the page as the Web author intended. Or close to it. Or maybe nothing like it at all.

You see, HTML has limitations in the way it displays information. It's important to know and understand these limitations when designing your Web pages.

- HTML was never intended to handle page layout. As a result, it's very difficult, if not downright impossible, to create a Web page that exactly replicates a complex print document such as a brochure.

- A Web page can be any length. It can also be any width. Word wrap is normally determined by the width of the Web browser window.  That means that changing the width of the browser window can change the appearance of a Web page in that window.

- Fonts appear larger in Windows  browsers than in Mac OS browsers. As a result, a page created by a Web author on a Mac OS system seems to have large fonts when viewed on Windows. Likewise, a page created by a Web author on Windows can have very tiny fonts when viewed on Mac OS.

- The fonts that can appear on a Web page are determined by the fonts installed on the site visitor's computer. So if you set up a page using fonts that the visitor doesn't have, text will appear in the default font. And the visitor can override special fonts anyway, to display all text in the font he prefers.

- Different Web browsers support different HTML tags. For example, Explorer supports the MARQUEE tag; Netscape does not. Similarly, Netscape supports the BLINK tag; Explorer does not. (Frankly, I find both of these tags rather annoying—and that's a better excuse for not using either one.)

- Older Web browsers do not support the most recent HTML tags. That means a Web page using HTML version 4.0 (the current version as I write this) won't look the same on an older browser (say, a Netscape or Explorer 2.0 browser) as it does on a current browser.

A smart Web author can overcome some of the limitations of HTML by intelligent coding. This, however, can cause other problems. For example, to fix the page width, all page information can be enclosed in a fixed-width borderless table. But this won't work for someone viewing the page with a very old browser. And if the width is fixed wider than the visitor's screen width, he'll have to scroll from side to side to see everything. (*No one* likes doing that.)

I guess the point I'm trying to make here is that you can't approach Web site or page design thinking that you'll have complete control over appearance. You won't. Instead of forcing your Web authoring software to imitate the tools available in page layout software, use the tools available within HTML to build pages that attractively and effectively communicate your message.

That's all you can do—and it's enough.

---

**MARKUP LANGUAGE**
A system of tags or codes that, when inserted with text and read with special software, displays formatted text, images, and other elements.

## Build a Company Image

Maybe your storefront or office isn't much different from that lawyer's reception area. Does that mean your Web site should be equally unimpressive? Of course not.

As I discussed back in Chapter 2, you can use your Web site as an image-building tool. Through the use of graphics, color, and writing style, you can make your Web site project the image you want to the people who visit.

Of course, a homegrown, amateurishly designed Web site can make your business look downright awful to visitors. Figure 7.1 shows an unnamed HVAC service company's Home page, which was created by the company's internal computer wiz. I touched up the screen shot to obscure the company name and contact info so the company wouldn't be embarrassed. Compare that to the Home page of The Chicago Safe Company (see Figure 2.5). I know that they're in different businesses, but which one would you be more likely to contact?

The sad thing (at least to me) is that more than half of the Web sites out there have a lot in common with this one. They were created by folks who don't know the first thing about design and the second thing about creating Web pages. Fortunately, these sites are seldom seen; this one has had only 52 hits in over a year and about 10 of those hits were from me showing people how ugly the site was.

## Using Graphic & Multimedia Elements Wisely

In my humble opinion, more Web sites have been ruined by the improper use of graphics than any other folly. In some instances, it's the result of having the site built by an amateur who couldn't design his way out of a paper bag. In other instances, it's the result of a talented designer being in love with graphics he can access at T1 speeds. It irritates the heck out of me and is the main reason I don't spend more time surfing the 'Net.

Let me calm down and explain.

## The Golden Rule

First, the golden rule of using images, graphics, and multimedia elements: the element must add something to the Web page without costing more than it's worth. Cost doesn't have anything to do with money. It has to do with how much time it takes for the element to appear in the visitor's Web browser window, how

FIGURE 7.1
An amateurishly designed Web site can make your company look bad. And if you think this looks bad, imagine it online where the diamond shaped bullets and "Page" links blink. Yuck.

FIGURE 7.1
An amateurishly designed Web site can make your company look bad. And if you think this looks bad, imagine it online where the diamond shaped bullets and "Page" links blink. Yuck.

much extra effort the visitor must spend to view the element (by downloading and installing plug-ins, etc.), and how annoyed the visitor might be that he wasted his time and effort to finally see the element.

*Every element you include on a Web page must be worth more than it costs.*

When evaluating worth and cost, you must be objective. Yes, it would be really cool if your Home page used a background image that was a photograph of your storefront. But how useful is it? Would visitors be able to read the text sitting on top of it? How much time would it take for the image to appear? If you want to show how beautiful your storefront is, wouldn't it be better to use a smaller image, possibly on the page where you provide your address and driving directions?

### Big is Bad

Ah, how I wish I could pound this concept into the head of Web designers all over the world. So many of them still don't get it.

Big images usually come with big file sizes. While it's possible to minimize file size by optimizing the image for Web use, there's only so much you can do. At the same time, a relatively small image that isn't optimized can also have an unnecessarily large file size.

At this point, you may be wondering what the big deal is. After all, your ISP may allow you 100 MBytes of hard disk space for your Web site. What's wrong with a few 100 Kbyte files?

There's nothing wrong with it as far as your ISP and Web server are concerned. It's the site visitor—remember? The person you're trying to provide information to?—who won't like it. You see, in order for an image to appear on a Web page, it must be downloaded from the Web server to the visitor's Web browser. The speed at which the image downloads is determined primarily by the speed of the visitor's connection to the Internet. Table 7.1 shows some typical image sizes and connection speeds with related download times.

**Table 7.1 Download Times for Various Image Sizes at Various Connection Speeds**

| | FILE SIZES & DOWNLOAD TIMES | | |
|---|---|---|---|
| **CONNECTION SPEEDS** | **5 KBYTES** | **25 KBYTES** | **100 KBYTES** |
| 28.8 Kbps | <1 sec | 8 secs | 34 secs |
| 33.6 Kbps | <1 sec | 7 secs | 29 secs |
| 56.8 Kbps | <1 sec | 4 secs | 17 secs |
| ISDN (128 Kbps) | <1 sec | <1 sec | 7 secs |
| T1 | <1 sec | <1 sec | 1 sec |

Now, someone using a modem to dial into his ISP—like most folks accessing the Internet from home—is likely to be connected at 28.8, 33.6, or 56.8 Kbps. So that 100 Kbyte file will take 34, 29, or 17 seconds to appear. Is the visitor likely to want to wait that long to see a picture of your storefront?

Studies have shown that the average Web surfer will wait less than 10 seconds for something interesting to appear on a Web page. If you fill your pages with fat images that take a long time to download, it isn't likely that the visitor will stick around to see your page at all.

### Multimedia Madness

Multimedia elements include animations, movies, and sounds. Like static images and graphic elements, they can make your site look more visually appealing and interesting. They can also provide information about your products, services, or company. But they can be very costly in terms of file size, download time, and convenience.

When multimedia effects are overdone or done incorrectly, they can make your site sluggish and unprofessional. If you surf the Web, I'm sure you've visited sites with pages that automatically load (or attempt to load) fancy animations or movies. Did you want to see that animation or movie? Maybe not. Yet it was forced on you when you went to the page. The Web designer assumed that you'd take the time to download and view it. (But you showed *him*. One look in the status bar to see how big the file was and you clicked the Back button and got out of there fast.)

*Multimedia elements (beyond simple quick-loading animations) should never be forced on a site's visitors.*

**TIP ▶** *If you do include large multimedia elements on your site, make them accessible by links. Clearly indicate the size of the file that will be downloaded when the link is clicked, as well as whether any special software is required to view it.*

### My Take on Sounds

Sound is another multimedia element that's often used incorrectly.

Here's an example. A center for bulemia and anorexia hired a Web designer to build a site with information about its main facility. The Web designer included music on the site's Home page, so when the Home page appeared, music would automatically play. Sounds neat, huh?

Not to everyone. Consider the worried mother who is at work, using her office computer on the sly to explore treatment options for her sick daughter. What do you think will happen when the sound of music starts coming out of her cubicle? Not only will her co-workers find out about a personal family problem, but she could be in danger of losing her job. Clearly, unexpected sounds should not be included on a Home page—or any other page, for that matter.

What's the proper use of sound? I can think of a few things. Obviously, if sound is part of your business—for example, if you're a musician or run a record company—it could be included on the site. Sound bytes can also be used to provide information—comments made by the company president at a recent press conference, for example. I'm sure you can think of other appropriate uses. But if you have to stretch your imagination to think of them for your business, they might not be appropriate after all.

**TIP ▶** *If you do decide to use sounds on your Web site, make them accessible by links. Clearly indicate that a sound will result when the link is clicked.*

### The Importance of Consistency

Does your company have a letterhead? Envelopes? Business cards? Do they all pretty much have the same design, complete with your company's logo?

They should. The consistent design of these basic printed materials helps enforce your company's identity. The inclusion of a company logo adds branding, further enforcing identity.

Your Web site should be the same. Not only should its overall design be consistent with your existing printed materials — including typefaces (when possible), colors, graphics, and logos — but each page should have the same basic design.

Consistency in appearance from one page to the next can help tie your site together. Once you develop an overall design for your site's Home page, you should use the same general design on the remaining pages. Then there's no question what site the visitor is viewing when he clicks a link. Either he's on another page of your site or he's on a different site altogether.

# Effective Navigation

Site navigation is an extremely important aspect of any Web site. After all, what good is a nice looking, information-packed Web site if visitors can't find the information they're looking for?

With effective site navigation, site visitors can find the information they need quickly and easily. They don't even have to *think* about where the information is or what they need to do to find it. By organizing information logically and including links to that information in appropriate places, site visitors should be able to intuitively navigate from one page to another to learn what they want to learn.

### Consider Usability

Usability refers to how effectively site visitors can access your site's information. It deals with concepts such as page design, element placement, and navigation.

Usability is part of what makes a Web site useful. It assures that information can be found without a lot of frustrating, time consuming site exploration. It also assures that when a user clicks a link (or something he thinks is a link), he won't be surprised or annoyed by what happens or appears.

*Usability is often ignored when designing Web sites. More Web designers seem concerned with creating a work of art than creating an effective, interactive way to present information. Don't fall into that trap. Remember who you are designing the Web site for—site visitors.*

**TIP ▶** *Want to learn more about usability and how it relates to Web sites? Check out* **Designing Web Usability,** *a New Riders Publishing book by Jakob Nielsen. Written primarily for Web design professionals, the book includes a wealth of information about how Web sites and pages can be designed to make them most effective. If all Web designers read this book, the Web would be a far more useful—and far less frustrating— place to get information.*

### The Three Click Rule

The Three Click Rule states that all content on your Web site should be within three clicks of the Home page. The idea is that site visitors shouldn't have to go digging for the information they need; it should be near the surface.

Here's how it works. Imagine a Web site for a florist who offers a wide variety of arrangements, including plants and flower baskets. A "Get Well Soon" arrangement is one of the products. A visitor might find that product by clicking a "Flowers" link on the Home page, then an "Arrangements" link on the Flowers page, and finally a "Get Well Soon" link on the Arrangements page. There's a logical flow of information there, created by a logical hierarchy.

*A logical hierarchy of information is, by far, the best way to organize a Web site.*

**Practicing What I Preach**

I can't remember where I first heard the Three Click Rule, but it stuck in my mind and I have made it a part of every Web site I've designed since then. But when I tried to think of an example from one of my sites for this book, I couldn't come up with one. I must use a Two Click Rule, because none of the pages on any of my sites are more than two clicks from the home page.

I used to believe that there was an exception to this rule, that it was okay to ignore it if you wanted to "force" site visitors to explore your site. I don't believe that anymore. There are two reasons:

○ It's impossible to "force" a site visitor to do anything. If you annoy someone enough, he'll just leave your site.

○ Your site should be built to serve the people who visit it by providing the information they expect to find. Making them wade through a lot of irrelevant information is selfish and shows no consideration for the people you're trying to serve.

## Just Say No to Splash Screens

I don't know about you, but when I arrive at a site's Home page, I expect to find information and navigation tools to help me find the data I need. I certainly don't expect to have my time wasted with some fancy graphic-filled page with a link labeled "Click Here to Enter."

That fancy page is called a *splash screen* and it's the biggest blight to hit the Web. Some Web designers think these pages are useful for providing a welcome message or introduction to the site. The only thing they're good for is wasting the visitor's time. Studies have shown that as soon as a visitor realizes a splash screen is appearing, they click to move on. If the page takes a long time to load and the "Click to Enter" link doesn't appear right away, the visitor is likely to go elsewhere. (I do it regularly.) Forcing a visitor to look at a useless page is downright inconsiderate.

## Navigation Bars

Navigation bars, or simply navbars, are a great way to incorporate intuitive navigation into a Web site. A navbar is a row of buttons or textual links that offer access to Web pages.

### Using Navbars

On a large site, the main navbar might offer access to major areas of the site, while secondary navbars appear on the pages within each area, offering access to individual pages. The Quicken.com Web site (**http://www.quicken.com/**) is a good example. As shown in Figure 7.2, the main navbar appears as tabs near the top of the page. Another navbar below it displays links to pages for the current "channel."

On a small site, a single navbar might offer access to all (or almost all) site pages. For example, the wickenburg-az.com Web site (**http://www.wickenburg-az.com/**) displays the same navbar, which offers access to most site pages, on every Web page (see Figure 7.3).

**FIGURE 7.2**
The Quicken.com Investing channel page includes two horizontal navbars at the top of the page.

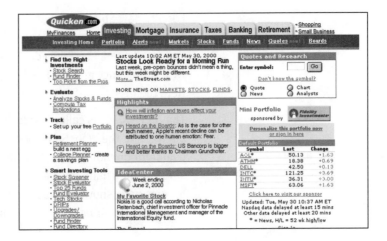

### Navbar Orientation

Navbars can be oriented horizonally or vertically. When oriented horizontally, they usually appear at the top of the Web page (see Figure 7.2), but can appear at the bottom or both at the bottom and top. When oriented vertically, they almost always appear on the left side of the page (see Figure 7.3).

### Positioning Navbars: Tables vs. Frames

To position a navbar vertically, it is usually included in either a table or a frame. Both of these structures are created within HTML.

A table is a structure built within a single page. Tables are used in many Web pages to create columns of information. In most cases, tables are borderless, so it isn't obvious that a table is used. Including a navbar in a table is a bit more work for the Web designer because it requires that he consistently create the navbar in every page that requires it.

A frame is created with a *frameset*—an arrangement of multiple Web pages within a single Web browser window. The navbar page is placed in its own frame of the frameset so it always appears in that position. Figure 7.3 shows an example of a navbar in a narrow vertical frame with frame borders disabled. If the navbar didn't fit in the frame, scroll bars could appear to enable the site visitor to scroll navbar contents. Although this is

**FIGURE 7.3**
The wickenburg-az.com Web site includes a vertical navbar that offers access to most pages.

a handy way to display the same navbar on every page, framesets are a bit more difficult to set up properly in HTML and frames are not as widely supported as tables.

### Image Map Navbars

Navbars can also be created using single images that are divided into multiple links. This uses the image map feature of HTML, where each clickable area is mapped to a specific URL. The main navbar in Figure 7.2 (the one with the tabs) was created with an image map.

The only drawback to using an image map is the size of the image and its download time. An image map should have a simple design and its image should be optimized so it loads quickly. Otherwise, the visitor has to wait for the links to appear.

### Breadcrumbs

Remember the story of Hansel and Gretel? They dropped breadcrumbs as they were led into the woods so they could find their way back home.

Breadcrumbs navigation on the Web works much the same way. It displays a path to the current page, with links to previous pages. This offers two benefits to site visitors:

o   Visitors can see where they are in relation to the site's hierarchy.

o   Visitors can quickly backtrack to any page along the path to the current page.

Figure 7.4 shows an example from one of my sites, wickenburg-az.com (http://www.wickenburg-az.com/). The breadcrumbs navigation feature appears at the top of the page, clearly showing the path to the current page. When viewed with the navbar along the left side of the page, it's clear how the current page fits into the site's hierarchy of information.

FIGURE 7.4
Breadcrumbs navigation usually
appears at or near the top of a Web
page, like it does on this one.

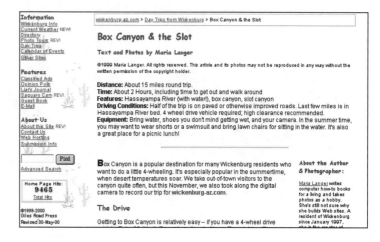

# Food for Thought

The information in this chapter should have gotten the wheels in your head turning, thinking about site design and what you can do to make it effective. Here are a few exercises to help you come up with a solid plan. To see what other readers think or to share your thoughts with them, visit the book's companion Web site at **http://www.smallbusinessonweb.com/**.

- Fire up your Web browser and go surfing. Visit ten sites you've never seen before. (You can start with your usual Home page, then click links to surf to new sites or use a search engine to find sites about a specific topic.) What do you like or dislike about the design of each site? How effective is site navigation?

- Consult the outline of site contents that you created in the previous chapter. If you used that outline to set up a hierarchy for your Web site, could you apply the Three Click Rule? If not, how could you change the outline to make the hierarchy more shallow?

- Think about navigation features you can include on your site. Which do you think are best for you? Why?

# CHAPTER EIGHT

# Saving Money by Doing It Yourself

Why pay a Web consultant or designer to build your Web site when you can do it yourself? In this chapter, I begin by explaining the basics of building a Web site, then go on to tell you about some popular, easy-to-use Web authoring tools for Mac OS and Windows users. I also provide a list of dos and don'ts that offers tips for doing the job right.

## In This Chapter

Building Web Pages: An Overview

Web Authoring Tools & Techniques

Tips for Doing It Right

# Building Web Pages: An Overview

Generally speaking, Web sites are made up of HTML documents—plain text documents that combine text and HTML tags or codes. Each HTML document makes up a Web page. A group of related (and usually linked) Web pages make up a Web site.

In this part of the chapter, I explain the basics of building a Web site. This information is vital if you plan to build a Web site yourself and want to do it right the first time. It'll also be very helpful if you hire a Web designer and want to understand what he is doing.

## A Closer Look at HTML

I introduced HTML back in Chapter 1. If you plan on creating Web pages, it's time to take a closer look at it.

HTML works by encoding plain text with HTML tags. By enclosing text within tags, you can specify how the text is to be formatted. You can also include path names or URLs within certain tags to display images or create links.

Figure 8.1 shows a very small, very simple Web page that combines text, images, and links. Figure 8.2 shows the HTML code that made up that page. Kind of scary, isn't it?

### Markup Languages, Programming Languages, & the Bottom Line for Web Authors

Web pages are created with a MARKUP LANGUAGE that is read and interpreted by Web browsers. There are several popular markup languages—HTML, DHTML, and XML are just three of them. But the one supported by all Web browsers is HTML. And as I write this, the current version of HTML is 4.0, which is fully supported by all current Web browsers, as well as some older ones.

Web pages can also be enhanced through the use of programming languages, such as Java and JavaScript. Unfortunately, these technologies are not as widely supported as HTML by Web browsers, so not all users can see content or features created with them.

The bottom line is this: a smart Web designer will create Web pages using HTML, and use less supported markup languages or programming languages for less important content or features. This can limit the features you include on your Web site, but if your Web designer knows what he's doing, he can get around the limitations of HTML to include the content and features you need the way you want them to appear on screen.

Fortunately, as you'll learn later in this chapter, you don't have to enter all those codes manually to create a Web page. In fact, you don't even have to know HTML at all—although a basic knowledge might be helpful for troubleshooting problems.

**FIGURE 8.1**
Here's an example of a very short, very simple Web page that includes formatted text, a graphic, and a link.

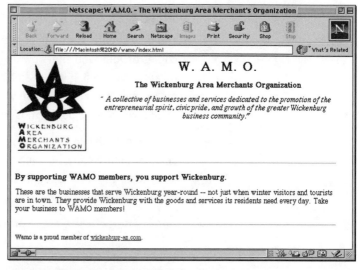

**FIGURE 8.2**
Here's the HTML underlying the above Web page.

## Building Locally, Uploading Remotely

When you create a Web site, you build it on your computer, not on the Web server. This is referred to as the *local* copy of your site. Then, when you are ready to put your site online, you upload it to the Web server. The Web server has the *remote* copy of your site.

You may already see a small problem with this. If you have two copies of your Web site, how do you know which one is the more recent copy? Well, if you're smart and organized, you'll only make changes to the copy on your computer—the local copy. Then it will always be the most up-to-date.

Of course, Web site visitors don't see the local copy. They only see the remote copy. So each time you make a change to the local copy, you must put a fresh copy on the Web server, thus updating the remote copy so it matches the local copy.

Here's a quick review of the process:

1.  Create the Web site locally.

2.  Upload the local copy of the Web site to the Web server to create a remote copy.

3.  Make changes as necessary to the local copy of the Web site.

4.  Upload the changed files in the local copy to the Web server to update the remote copy.

I'll tell you more about uploading files to a Web server in Chapter 10.

## Organizing Files

When you create the local copy of your Web site, it's important to properly organize the files that will make up the site. This way, when you copy the local files to the Web server, the files will retain their relationships to one another. This assures that all links will function correctly and all images will appear as they should.

Here's a step-by-step approach to organizing your Web site's files on your hard disk.

### Step 1: Create & Name the Local Root Folder

Begin by creating a folder in which to store the local copy of your Web site on your hard disk. This folder is called the *local root* folder because it will be at the root directory of your Web site.

You can name this folder anything you like, but I usually give it the same name as the folder in which the remote copy of the Web site will reside. For example, my local copy of the files for wickenburg-az.com is named *wickenburg* because that's the same name as the site's folder on the Web server.

### Step 2: Create & Name Resource Folders

Resources are Web site files other than HTML documents. Resources include images, downloadable files, PDF format files, Java class files (if Java is used), and any other type of file that is used within an HTML document.

If your site will have only a few resources, one folder should do the job. Name it anything you like—*resources* isn't a bad name.

If your site is likely to have lots of different types of resources, you might want to create a folder for each type. For example, wickenburg-az.com's site includes graphic images, photographs, and PDF format files. To best organize all of these files, I created folders called *images*, *photos*, and *pdfs*.

On the other hand, if your site will be so tiny that it's likely to include only a handful of files, including resources, you can skip this step.

### Step 3: Create & Name Subfolders (Optional)

If your Web site will be very large, with a logical, hierarchical organization, you may want to create additional folders within the root folder in which to store groups of related Web pages. There are two benefits to doing this:

○ **SUBFOLDERS HELP YOU KEEP WEB PAGES ORGANIZED BY TOPIC.** This makes it easier for you to manage HTML and related resources files.

○ **SUBFOLDERS HELP THE SITE VISITOR UNDERSTAND WHERE THE PAGE HE IS VIEWING FITS INTO THE SITE'S ORGANIZATIONAL HIERARCHY.** How? Well, the URL that appears in the Address or Location area at the top of the Web browser window includes the path from the root folder to the current document (see Figure 8.3).

**FIGURE 8.3**
The path to a page's location on disk appears near the top of the Web browser window.

If each group of Web pages has its own collection of resources, you might consider creating resources folders within each subfolder. This can further aid your organization efforts if there are many files.

## File Naming Conventions

Before you begin creating and saving Web pages, you should check with your ISP for any special file naming conventions. File name requirements are determined by the Web server, not the computer on which you create the files.

Specifically, ask these three questions:

○ **ARE FILENAME EXTENSIONS ON A 3-CHARACTER SYSTEM OR A 4-CHARACTER SYSTEM?** You'll either be required to stick to 3-character extensions (such as .htm, .gif, and .jpg) or you'll be allowed 3- or 4-character extensions (such as .html, .gif, and .jpg). No matter what, a filename extension or suffix will be required— Web browsers use them to identify types of files.

- ○ **WHAT IS THE FILENAME OF THE DEFAULT PAGE?** The default page is the file that's automatically served if someone enters a URL that does not include a filename. In most cases, this will be your Home page's name. The default page filename is normally one of the following: *index.html*, *index.htm*, *default.html*, or *default.htm*.

- ○ **IS THE WEB SERVER CASE SENSITIVE?** On some servers, Index.html is not the same as index.html. If the server is case-sensitive, you must know before you start saving files and creating links. Otherwise, if the pathnames to files you link to do not have the correct case, your links won't work.

One thing I can tell you so you don't have to ask is that filenames cannot include spaces.

If you don't get the answers to these questions before you start creating pages and you name them incorrectly, you'll have to rename pages and recreate links. Trust me, this is *not* something you want to do.

## Creating Pages

When you're ready to begin creating Web pages for your site, fire up your Web authoring software of choice and hop to it.

Unfortunately, I can't provide detailed instructions for creating Web pages, because the task varies depending on the Web authoring software you use.

If you're brand new to building Web sites, I recommend that you work through any tutorial that may have come with your Web authoring software. If there isn't a tutorial, use the manual that came with the software to create simple pages. You can always get fancy later, once you have a good handle on how the software works. If there isn't a manual, get a how-to guide; there's a good chance it'll be better than any manual anyway.

**TIP ▶** *I tell you about Web authoring software and some how-to guides to get the most of it later in this chapter.*

## Adding Resources & Links

Adding resources (such as images) and links to pages can be tricky. If you're going to have problems, this is probably where they'll occur.

Here are a few things to remember if you want to prevent resource and link-related problems.

- Always save a Web page file before inserting resources or creating links to other pages within it. Save the file in the correct location with the correct name.

- Create and save resources within the appropriate resources folder *before* creating links to them.

- Avoid letting the Web authoring software create and save image files for you. In many cases, the software will save the image in the wrong disk location with a generic name that makes the image hard to find or identify.

- Do not move or rename a resource after it has been inserted in a Web page. Doing so will invalidate the reference to the resource within the Web page and the resource will not appear.

- Do not move or rename a link's destination page. Doing so will invalidate the link.

*References to resources and links to other pages within your site are usually created relative to the page on which the link resides. That's why you should avoid renaming or moving resources and pages on your site.*

## Testing Pages

An important (and overlooked) part of building a Web site is testing the completed Web pages. This means opening them up with a Web browser—or better yet, multiple Web browsers—to make sure they appear and work the way they should. If something isn't right, use your Web authoring software to fix it (if you can) and test it again.

Using the preview feature of your Web authoring software to test a Web page is usually not enough. Only by looking at a page in a Web browser window can you be certain how it will look in that Web browser.

**TIP ▶** *If possible, try testing each Web page with a variety of Web browsers—including old browsers—on a variety of computer systems and screen sizes. You may be surprised how different the same page can appear when viewed with different software or computer systems (see Figure 8.4).*

The testing process must be repeated every time you make a change to a Web page. If you think that could get tedious, you're very astute. But testing is the only way to assure that the page is just right.

# Web Authoring Tools & Techniques

Now that you know the general steps required to build your Web site, it's time to take a look at the tools and techniques you can use to get the job done.

The way I see it, there are two ways to go about creating Web pages: the hard way and the easy way.

### The Hard Way: Editing Raw HTML

The hard way to create a Web page is by typing HTML tags and text into a text editor or word processor. If you take another look at Figure 8.2, you can get an idea of the kind of fun that would be.

**FIGURE 8.4**

These two pages show the same page viewed with a variety of browsers, screen sizes, and computer platforms. Although the page doesn't look the same in every shot, it doesn't "break"— look terrible or illegible in any of these combinations.

This page:

Top: Mac OS, Netscape Navigator 2.0, 640 x 480 screen. This version does not support style sheets, so the default font is used.

Middle: Mac OS, Netscape Communicator 4.7, 640 x 480 screen.

Bottom: Mac OS, Netscape Communicator, 600 x 800 screen.

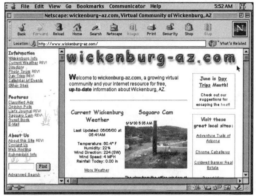

FIGURE 8.4 (CONTINUED)
This page:
Top: Windows 95, Microsoft Internet
Explorer, 640 x 480 screen.
Middle: Windows 95, Microsoft Internet
Explorer, 600 x 800 screen.
Bottom: Windows 95, Netscape
Navigator 4.0, 600 x 800 screen.

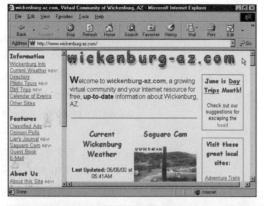

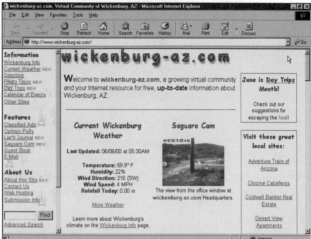

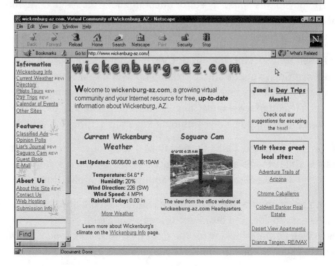

*To edit raw HTML, you need to know HTML. There are lots of books that can help you learn it, but one of the best for beginners is* HTML 4 for the World Wide Web: Visual QuickStart Guide, *a Peachpit Press book by Elizabeth Castro. You can learn more about it at http://www.peachpit.com/ books/catalog/K5950.html.*

If you know HTML and want to build Web pages the old fashioned way, you don't need special software. Any text editor—such as WordPad on Windows or SimpleText on Mac OS—will work. You could also use a word processor capable of saving documents as plain text—like Microsoft Word. Just remember to save the finished HTML document with the correct filename extension: *.html* or *.htm*.

## The Easy Way: Web Authoring Software

It may come as a surprise to you, but back when I started building Web sites in 1995, editing raw HTML was the only way to create a Web page. Then a little program called PageMill hit the scene. It revolutionized the way Web authors created pages

### They're Not Dead Yet!

When I proposed this book, my editor questioned my inclusion of Adobe PageMill and Claris Home Page as two of the Web authoring software packages I'd mention. She, like so many other people, questioned the continued life of these two products.

When Adobe Systems, Inc. bought GoLive, Inc., doomsayers proclaimed the death of PageMill. But PageMill and GoLive peacefully co-existed for over a year. These two products are for different markets; PageMill is for the entry level Web author while GoLive is for more advanced Web designers who can figure out its complex interface—something I've never been able to do. In the summer of 2000, Adobe officially announced that it would be discontinuing PageMill, although it would still support PageMill users.

FileMaker, Inc. (formerly Claris Corporation) discontinued development on Home Page in 1999, but the program is still listed as a current product on FileMaker, Inc.'s Web site. And I don't care what anyone says: for creating FileMaker Pro custom Web publishing solutions, Home Page can't be beat.

These two programs are excellent choices for new Web authors because they're affordable (under $100), extremely easy to use, and they keep things simple with basic HTML that will work in any browser. My advice to Web newbies looking for the right Web authoring tool: If you see either one of these programs (preferably PageMill) buy it. You'll get your money's worth and more.

by offering **WYSIWYG** editing. You'd build a Web page with a word processor-like interface and PageMill would write all the HTML code for you.

Nowadays there are several software packages that do pretty much the same thing. Here's a quick look at them, along with information about where you can learn more.

### Adobe PageMill

Adobe PageMill was the first of the WYSIWYG Web authoring packages and it still has a loyal user base. It's a great package for beginners because it's intuitive and extremely easy to use (see Figure 8.5). Its built-in SITE MANAGEMENT and FTP capabilities, along with a "lite" version of Adobe Photoshop, make it an affordable solution for most basic Web authoring needs.

PageMill doesn't support all of HTML 4.0 (the current version), but it does allow you to edit the HTML it writes to add unsupported tags and features. This makes PageMill reasonably powerful in the hands of someone who knows HTML.

*Until recently, PageMill was my primary Web authoring tool.*

Although PageMill has been officially discontinued by Adobe Systems (see sidebar "They're Not Dead Yet!"), you may still find it in stores or mail order catalogs. Learn more about it on the PageMill pages of the Adobe Systems Web site, http://www.adobe.com/products/pagemill/main.html.

> **TIP ▶** *If you're looking for a great book about using PageMill, I hope you'll check out* PageMill 3 for Macintosh & Windows: Visual QuickStart Guide, *a Peachpit Press book by yours truly. You can learn more about it at http://www.peachpit.com/books/catalog/K5900.html.*

**WYSIWYG**
Stands for What You See Is What You Get. For Web authoring software, a feature that enables you to see how a Web page will look as you edit it.

**SITE MANAGEMENT**
A feature of some Web authoring software that enables you to view and work with the organizational hierarchy of a Web site.

FIGURE 8.5
PageMill's Edit mode offers a word
processor-like interface for creating Web
pages.

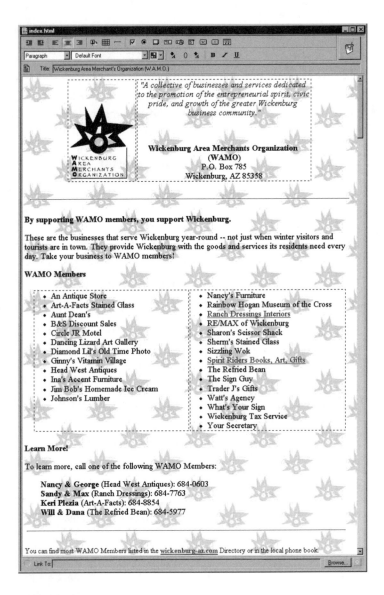

## FileMaker Home Page (formerly Claris Home Page)

Claris Home Page was another one of the original WYSIWYG Web authoring packages. Since then, Claris Corporation has been dissolved back into Apple Computer, Inc. and Home Page was spit back out as part of the product line of the newly formed FileMaker, Inc.

Like PageMill, Home Page doesn't support all of HTML 4.0, but it does offer built-in HTML editing. It has FTP capabilities, but not site management tools. As a Web authoring tool, it would probably have died by now if it wasn't for one great feature: built-in support for FileMaker Pro custom Web publishing commands known as Claris Dynamic Markup Language (CDML). This makes Home Page an indispensable tool for putting FileMaker Pro databases on the Web.

Home Page is available for both Windows and Mac OS users. You can learn more about it on the Home Page pages of the FileMaker, Inc. Web site, **http://www.filemaker.com/products/ hp_home.html.**

**TIP ▶** *Looking for a book about Home Page? Try* **Claris Home Page 3 for Windows & Macintosh: Visual QuickStart Guide,** *a Peachpit Press book by Richard Fenno. To my knowledge, this is the only book available about the program. Learn about it at http://www.peachpit.com/books/catalog/69647.html.*

### Microsoft FrontPage

Microsoft FrontPage is the third of the original three WYSIWYG Web authoring tools. Like PageMill, it offers an easy way to create Web pages, along with site management and FTP capabilities. But unlike PageMill, it supports all the current Web technologies, including HTML 4.0, DHTML, JavaScript, and more. That's a double-edged sword; if Page Options are not properly set for each Web page, it's possible to create pages that include Microsoft server-specific codes which may not work on your server.

FrontPage is available for both Windows and Mac OS users— with a catch. The Mac OS version has not been updated since its original release several years ago so it lacks most of the features available in the Windows version. For this reason, I do not recommend the Macintosh version of FrontPage.

You can learn more about FrontPage for Windows on the FrontPage pages of the Microsoft Corporation Web site, http://www.microsoft.com/frontpage/.

**TIP ▶** *Another program, another Visual QuickStart Guide. For FrontPage, try* FrontPage 2000 for Windows: Visual Quick-Start Guide, *a Peachpit Press book by Nolan Hester. Learn more about it at http://www.peachpit.com/books/catalog/K5914.html.*

## Macromedia Dreamweaver

Oddly enough, when Dreamweaver first appeared at computer shows, it did not include a WYSIWYG editing tool. Instead, it's main focus was on site management and the Web designer was required to code in HTML. (This was back in the days right after WYSIWYG Web authoring programs first came out and some silly purists insisted that raw HTML editing was the "right" way to create Web pages.)

Nowadays, Macromedia Dreamweaver has both WYSIWYG and HTML editing. (What's really cool is that you can view both the WYSIWYG window and the HTML window at the same time, make changes in one, and see the effect of those changes

### Microsoft's Other Web Authoring Tools: Publisher & Word

Microsoft does offer two other programs that can create Web pages, but I'm not sure I'd recommend either one. Here's the scoop:

○ Microsoft Word is a word processor with the ability to save formatted documents as HTML documents. It does this by writing HTML code when you save the document. Although this isn't bad for creating quick and dirty Web pages to put information on the Web in a hurry, I don't consider it a serious Web authoring tool. You shouldn't either, no matter what Microsoft's marketing material might say.

○ Microsoft Publisher is a page layout package that also has the ability to save documents as HTML. How it does this, however, is rather frightening: it creates huge graphics for the text and images that make up the Web page. As a result, the pages it creates take a very long time to appear in Web browser windows. From what I've seen, once they do appear, they're usually not worth waiting for.

Would you use a corkscrew to open a can? Personally, I'd use a can opener. That's what they're for.

immediately in the other; see Figure 8.6.) It still has great site management tools, as well as both upload and download FTP capabilities. It supports all of the current Web authoring technologies and is extensible through the use of "objects" that can be added to the program. (Many of these objects are available for free right on the Macromedia Web site.)

Dreamweaver is not for everyone. It's a bit advanced for new Web designers, although its relatively intuitive interface makes it easy to use. It's the kind of program that can grow with your Web authoring skills—but it can also get you in trouble if you don't know what you're doing.

*Dreamweaver has become my Web authoring tool of choice. I can't say enough good things about this program.*

Dreamweaver is available for Windows and Macintosh. You can learn more about it on the Dreamweaver pages of the

**FIGURE 8.6**
Dreamweaver is a full-featured WYSIWYG authoring program that supports all of the current Web technologies.

Macromedia Web site, http://www.macromedia.com/software/ dreamweaver/.

**TIP ▶** *If you're looking for a book about Dreamweaver, try*
*Dreamweaver 3 for Windows & Macintosh: Visual QuickStart*
*Guide, a Peachpit Press book by J. Tarin Towers. You can learn*
*all about it at http://www.peachpit.com/books/catalog/*
*70240.html.*

### Adobe GoLive

GoLive is another powerful, feature-packed Web authoring program. Originally developed as GoLive Cyberstudio by GoLive, Inc., it joined the Adobe family of products when Adobe Systems, Inc. bought GoLive. One name change and two revisions later, it's a popular package among professional Web designers.

GoLive includes Web authoring, site management, and FTP capabilities. It supports all the current Web technologies, making it a good tool for building Web sites with the latest and greatest features. The guy who shows off the product at computer shows gives a great demo that has the audience drooling. Unfortunately, the program's interface is far from intuitive and, when you get the product home, you wonder how he did it.

*GoLive is one of the few software programs I've never been able to learn, despite tutorials, manuals, and other learning aids. Either it's difficult to learn or I have some kind of mental block against it.*

GoLive is available for both Windows and Mac OS. You can learn more about it on the Go Live pages of the Adobe Systems Web site, http://www.adobe.com/products/golive/main.html.

**TIP** ▶ *You'll need a good book about Go Live if you plan to master it. Try one or both of these:*

- **Adobe GoLive 4 for Macintosh & Windows: Visual QuickStart Guide,** *a Peachpit Press book by Shelly Brisbin. Learn about it at http://www.peachpit.com/ books/catalog/K5934.html.*

- **Adobe GoLive 4 Classroom in a Book,** *an Adobe Press book by the Adobe Creative Team. Learn about it at http://www.peachpit.com/books/catalog/L7694.html.*

*New versions of these books may be available by the time you read this.*

### Others

There are other WYSIWYG Web authoring packages out there. The ones I've mentioned here are just the most popular of the bunch. Check the Web sites for your favorite software catalog stores to see what's available. Then visit the sites of the software developers to get more information and trial versions.

# Tips for Doing It Right

Well, without getting product-specific, that's about all the instruction I can give you for building your own Web site...except these few words of advice and reminders.

### Words of Wisdom from Someone Who's Been There

In 1995, I was a freelance writer and Macintosh consultant with a few good clients. When one of them decided to build a Web presence, I had a choice: learn about the Web so I could provide a new service or lose the client to another consultant who could do it all. I decided to learn about the Web.

Here are the things I learned about Web authoring when I first started out:

- **USE WEB SITE DESIGN AIDS.** Many Web authoring programs include templates or assistants for creating Web pages and sites. Use them as a starting point, then customize the pages to fine-tune them for your needs.

- **BROWSE OTHER SITES AND SOURCES TO GET IDEAS.** (I can't stress this enough!) Maybe you're not in the design business, but that doesn't mean you don't know what looks good. Check out other sites and take notes about the things you see that you like. Then incorporate them into your site.

- **STUDY UP WITH REFERENCE GUIDES.** If you skipped Chapters 5 through 7, shame on you! They offer a lot of useful information to help you plan and design your site. But this book shouldn't be your only reference. I mention other books throughout this one—check the Reading List in Appendix A for a complete list. Some of those books may also help you get the job done.

- **BE LEGIBLE.** Busy background images make text difficult to read. Text and background colors should contrast well to be legible. Avoid teeny tiny print. Use font styles, headings, and lists to increase legibility and set off key points.

## Don't Forget To…

I've said these things elsewhere in this book, but they're important enough to repeat here:

- **USE EXISTING COMPANY LOGOS AND GRAPHICS.** Company design elements like logos, graphics, and text set in certain typefaces can extend the company identity to the Web site. If these elements don't already exist in electronic form, they can be scanned in and coverted to GIF or JPEG images for use on the Web.

- **KEEP GRAPHIC FILE SIZES SMALL.** Remember, not everyone wants to wait for your images to load. The Back button, Address bar, and bookmarks menu are well within mouse pointer reach. You've got less than ten seconds to attract and keep the attention of a site visitor. Don't blow it on big graphics!

- **PROVIDE VALUABLE CONTENT.** If you don't provide the information that visitors want, they won't come back for more. Include product, service, and company information. Look in company catalogs and brochures for ideas of what to include. Remember, if 1,000 people get this information from the Web, that's 1,000 fewer catalogs and brochures you'll have to print and distribute the old fashioned way.

- **REMEMBER THE THREE CLICK RULE.** All important information on your Web site should be within three clicks of the Home page. Don't bury the information that site visitors want!

- **BE TASTEFUL.** Your Web site is like a virtual place of business. Would you paint your walls lime green and put up day-glo orange signs? Don't use irritating colors and tasteless graphics—unless they're part of your company identity. (And, if they are, perhaps it's time for an identity change?)

- **TEST YOUR PAGES.** Preview your completed Web pages with a variety of Web browsers—including older ones—with a variety of screen widths. Preview them on other computer systems, too, if you can. That's the only way to know for sure what your Web pages will look like in visitors' browsers.

- **KEEP YOUR SITE UP TO DATE.** Old news is bad news. If visitors see the same old information each time they visit the site, they'll stop visiting. Update the Home page regularly. Prominently display news and valuable information so visitors immediately see the value of visiting the site regularly.

# Food for Thought

It's time to think about the information covered in this chapter. Here are a few suggestions for getting the thought processes going. To see what others have come up with or to share your thoughts with other readers, be sure to visit the companion Web site for this book, http://www.smallbusinessonweb.com/.

- Think about the concept of building your Web site locally and then uploading a copy to the Web server. What are some of the other benefits to doing this? What are some of the drawbacks?

- Look at the Web site hierarchy you worked on in the previous two chapters. Use it to create a local root folder with subfolders on your hard disk. (Or simply write down the names of folders and subfolders you think you'll need.)

- Can you think of any reason you might want to learn HTML in preparation for creating a Web site?

- What's more important to you in a software package: ease of use or power?

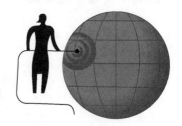

# CHAPTER NINE

# Working with a Web Designer

Let's face it: not everyone has what it takes to design an effective, professional-looking Web site. If you don't think you're up to the job, it's a good idea to hire a Web designer. This chapter explains how you can find a good Web designer and make sure his ideas are in sync with yours. It then provides tips for communicating with the designer and making sure you stay in control of your site.

## In This Chapter

# Finding a Web Designer

You've decided to hire a Web designer and you want to make sure you find and choose the right person for the job. Great! This part of the chapter will help you find candidates for the position and "interview" them so you know they can do the job you want for the price you're willing to pay.

## Where to Look

There are a number of resources you can check to begin your search for a Web designer. Here's a quick overview of the ones I think are best, so you can see the benefits and drawbacks of each. I recommend that you use all the resources you can when making a list of candidates.

### Phone Book

Your local phone book's Yellow Pages should have listings for Web designers. Look under the *Internet* category. The Wickenburg area phone book (which is, admittedly, very small) has subcategories for *Internet Consultants* and *Internet Web Site Developers*. (Of course, both of those subcategories are empty in the Wickenburg area phone book, but just seeing them there is very promising.)

### Web Designer/Author/Developer/Consultant

If you've been paying very close attention, you may have noticed that I've been using several titles interchangeably: Web designer, Web author, Web developer, and Web consultant. That's because although I can make a distinction between these titles, it isn't much of a distinction. These people all do pretty much the same thing: they design and create Web sites.

To avoid confusion (and keep my editor from marking up this chapter with her red pencil), I'll stick to one title throughout this chapter: Web designer. Just keep in mind that when you hire a Web designer, he might use any of the titles I've been throwing around in this book—or he might even use the one I like: Internet Content Creator.

One more thing: A Webmaster can also design and create Web sites, but he's usually more concerned with the day-to-day job of keeping the site up and running.

Unless you live on the edge of nowhere, like I do, your phone book should list several possibilities in the basic listings and in large display ads. Here's my take on those:

- Big display ads are usually placed by businesses that are serious about advertising. They have a big advertising budget, which could mean they're successful. But it could also mean that they charge a lot for their services or that they're desperate for clients.

- Basic listing ads are usually placed by businesses who aren't too concerned about advertising or have small advertising budgets. This could mean that they're not doing well enough to afford more. But it could also mean that they're so successful they don't need a bigger ad.

If you're in a big city, you might want to start with the Web designers who are located closest to you. A nearby location can make meetings convenient and it can sure cut transportation costs if your Web designer bills for it.

## Newspaper

The local newspaper may also be a good source of leads for Web designers. If your paper has a technology or computer section, that's the best place to look. Look for ads that provide a lot of information about the Web designer's services.

Don't look in the classified ads section. Classified ads are for selling cars, renting apartments, and finding jobs. A Web designer who advertises with classified ads probably isn't worth the amount of money he spent to place the ad.

## Friends & Business Associates

If you have friends or business associates who have built a Web presence, ask who they used to get the job done. Not only will you get a name and phone number, but you'll get honest opinions about the work done.

Be sure to ask what they thought of the Web developer's work and ability to satisfy their needs. If they used someone who got the job done, but not without problems, you might want to avoid using the same person. After all, you want the process to be as trouble-free as possible, right?

### Your ISP

Chances are, your ISP has a staff of Web designers or works with a pool of Web designers who can handle your needs. In fact, most ISPs have Web site packages that include everything you need to get your Web site online.

Talk to your ISP to see what it has to offer. Or, if you haven't selected an ISP yet, make sure you review available Web design services before you choose one.

---

*Don't be lazy and use your ISP's staff to handle your Web development needs without exploring other options first. Just because it's convenient, doesn't mean it's good.*

---

### Online

Another way to find a Web designer is by checking the Web. There are three ways you can do this:

#### One-Stop Shopping at Your ISP? Think Again

ISPs are in the business of selling Internet services, especially services that can billed on an ongoing basis. The predefined packages many ISPs offer may include services that you don't need. But because the ISP's Web designer is in the ISP's camp, he won't objectively advise you about the ISPs services.

Here's a true story. A friend of mine's father runs a small, one-man business. He hired an ISP and its Web designer to build him a Web site. They sold him a "Silver" package (or some similar bogus name) that included domain name registration, setup, Web hosting for a 60 MB Web site, 10 e-mail addresses, and monthly maintenance. Then they built him a three-page Web site that is less than 200 K in size and set up one e-mail address for him. He paid thousands of dollars to set the thing up and pays about $1,000 a year for Web hosting and "maintenance." He doesn't get what he paid for because he doesn't need it. But because he didn't have an objective advisor to tell him what he needed (the "Lead" package, if there was one, should have done it), he bought and paid for far more than he'll ever use.

Don't let this happen to you.

- USE SEARCH ENGINES. Try any of the titles that might apply, one at a time. Or try something more generic, like Web creation services. You'll wind up with a whopping big list of Web developers and ISPs to choose from. (The ones at the top of the list are good at getting themselves found by search engines; something you might want to consider as a plus.) Follow links to learn more.

- CONSULT WEB-BASED DIRECTORIES. The Web Design List on Internet.com (**http://www.designlist.internet.com/**; see Figure 9.1) is a good example. It has a searchable database of Web designers. You can specify a location, as well as the types of services you'll need to build your site.

- SURF THE WEB TO FIND SITES YOU LIKE, THEN FIND OUT WHO CREATED THEM. After all, as you explore the Web, you probably see many sites that make you think "I wish my Web site looked like that." Contact the owner or Webmaster of the site to get in touch with the Web designer.

## What to Ask

Once you have a list of candidates, it's time to interview them. Yes, I did say "interview." If the person you select is going to work for you, he should be interviewed like any other employee. In fact, he should probably be interviewed more thoroughly because he'll probably be paid more than most of your employees.

If one of your candidates is an organization (rather than an individual), it's important to gather information about the person or people who will actually be doing the work. Don't let some well-dressed, smooth-talking salesperson talk you into a relationship with his company unless you get facts about the Web designer who will be assigned to your job.

### Experience

One of the first questions you should ask a Web designer candidate is how long he's been designing Web sites. If the

FIGURE 9.1

The Web Design List at Internet.com offers a searchable database of Web designers all over the world.

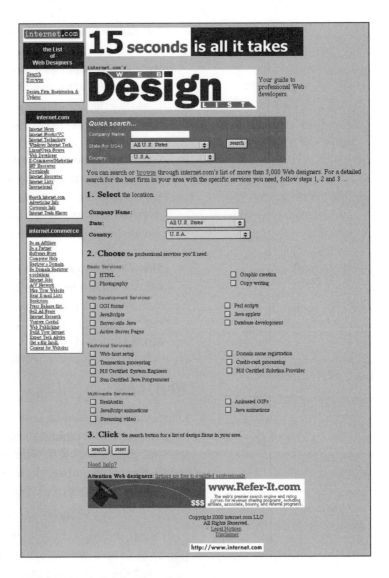

## Internet.com

Internet.com (http://www.internet.com/) is a very useful site for anyone interested in building a Web presence. Most of the information on the site is intended for Internet professionals, but there are many lists and links that the average small business owner or manager may find useful when putting his business on the Web.

answer is less than a year, let someone else give him the experience he needs to know what he's doing.

Here's another true story. I wrote a book about PageMill called *PageMill 3 for Macintosh & Windows: Visual QuickStart Guide*. One of the book's readers tracked me down via e-mail to ask me a few questions. It seemed he'd decided to learn PageMill so he could go into the Web design business. He had some questions about the Internet and how to get sites online, as well as how he could promote himself as a Web designer. And oh, by the way, could I recommend him to the clients I couldn't handle?

This story is scary on multiple levels. First of all, if you read Chapter 8, you should realize that PageMill is an entry level Web authoring program. Although it can make fine Web pages, it's extremely basic and has many limitations. A professional Web designer would not select it as a primary authoring tool unless he was prepared to spend a lot of time editing the HTML that PageMill created. Second, this new PageMill user felt that he knew everything he needed to know to build Web sites for other people. The sad truth is, he didn't even know enough to get his own Web site online. And I won't even begin to discuss his belief that I'd recommend him—a complete stranger—to do Web development work!

The point is, there are many people out there selling themselves as Web designers when, in fact, they know just enough to make them dangerous. Don't let one of them work on your Web site.

**Examples of Work**

Once you're convinced that the Web designer has been doing his job for a while, the next step is to see examples of his work. Fire up your Web browser and visit some sites he's created. He should be able to provide you with the URLs of at least ten sites that are on the Web. If he can't, ask him why. Could it be that he's never really created any Web sites for clients? This is a good way to see if he was lying about his experience.

*Don't settle for looking at screen shots of Web pages or sites the Web designer has stored on his computer. Insist on examples that are live, on the Web.*

While you're looking at his work, pay attention to a few things:

○ **IS THERE VARIETY IN OVERALL APPEARANCE FROM ONE SITE TO ANOTHER?** A good Web designer should be able to build sites that look different for each client. If all the sites have the same general appearance, the designer may try to apply his formula to your business's site—and the formula might not be appropriate.

○ **DO THE SITES LOAD QUICKLY ON YOUR INTERNET CONNECTION?** Many Web designers don't test their pages on slower connections. As a result, they don't load as quickly as they should. Remember, you don't want your customers or clients to wait too long for your Web site's information to appear.

○ **DO THE SITES SEEM APPROPRIATE FOR THE BUSINESSES THEY PROMOTE?** Look at content and features, as well as the use of design and navigation elements.

○ **DO THE SITES PROVIDE USEFUL INFORMATION USING NAVIGATION FEATURES THAT ARE EASY TO USE?** Look for gaps in information and information that is buried or hard to find.

○ **WOULD YOU BE PROUD TO HAVE A SITE LIKE THE ONES THE WEB DESIGNER HAS CREATED?** Remember, a Web site represents your business to the online world.

*If your Web site is a virtual place of business, the Web designer is the interior decorator.*

### Design Philosophy

Ask the Web designer what his design philosophy is. If he looks at you with crossed eyes, he probably hasn't thought much about it. He may even think you're nuts. But this is a legitimate question, one a real designer should be able to answer.

Whatever he says, it's important that it is similar to your philosophy. Otherwise, you'll have nothing but trouble during the design phase.

**TIP ▶** *Be sure to check out the Web designer's own Web site. This is the best indication of his personal philosophy about Web design.*

Ready for another true story? Until very recently (yesterday, in fact), I did some Web design work for the friend of a friend—I'll call him Tim. Tim hired me to build a Web site to promote his business. Once the bulk of the work was done, he'd modify and update the site using PageMill. I had no problem with that; I don't really have much time for Web design work these days anyway. So I went to work.

I'm not a real designer, but I do have a Web design philosophy (which you should have picked up from this book by now). I believe in simplicity, providing good information, and making that information easy to find. I also believe that a Web site should look good and that its pages should load quickly and be easy to read.

You probably know what's coming, but here it is. I designed a site for Tim to his specifications regarding pages and content. But then he started asking me to tweak the appearance. We made some changes that I wasn't comfortable with but that he seemed to like. Then the site went online and he took over. He inserted dozens of large photographs in the pages, increasing download times—one page took over two minutes to load! He reduced the font size, making it difficult to read the text. The page design was all but destroyed. He also complained that his site wasn't getting enough hits, but refused to let me add it to search engines and directories.

When I tried to point out the problems to Tim and offered to fix them, Tim got defensive. When I asked another Web designer to give Tim some objective feedback about the site, Tim got offensive. That's when I should have quit. But I backed down then; it was only after more of the same that I finally pulled the plug.

The moral of this story is this: If your design philosophy doesn't match the Web designer's design philosophy, one of you is going to be very unhappy. Let's hope it isn't you.

### Fees

Most people ask about fees first. I don't. But I do agree they're important to know up front.

Find out how the Web designer will bill you for the project. Does he bill based on an hourly rate or does he have some kind of package deal for a site? What's included in the fee? What's not included in the fee and what do those things cost?

A professional Web designer should be able to give you a written estimate for the project. This document should discuss what is and isn't included and note whether the amounts are binding or simply estimates. (Get binding estimates whenever possible to avoid surprises.)

**TIP ▶** *If a Web designer is vague about his fees, don't hire him. You should know all about costs before you hire a designer.*

*Finally, don't select a Web designer just because he's the cheapest you could find. You get what you pay for.*

### References

If everything the Web designer has said up to this point is right in line with what you want, it's time to ask for references. These references should be clients for whom the Web designer has built sites within the past year. They should also be sites that you have seen among the Web designer's examples of his work.

Get at least two references. Then, when the interview is over, call them. Here are a few things you could ask:

o   Was the Web designer easy to work with?

o   Did the Web designer meet the client's needs?

o   Was the Web designer receptive to change requests?

- Was the Web designer able to effectively communicate information about content, features, and design?

- Did the Web designer finish the work when he said he would?

- Was the Web designer's fee in line with original estimates?

- Would the client recommend the Web designer to others?

The answers to these questions should provide a good indication of the Web designer's level of professionalism and ability to satisfy the client's needs.

### Hire Him!

Once you've made your decision, hire the Web designer you've selected.

Get the relationship off on the right foot by creating a document that summarizes what the Web designer will do for you, when it should be done, and approximately what it will cost. In many cases, an existing estimate will do the job nicely. Make sure that you both sign the document and keep a copy. This will form the basis of your working relationship.

# Staying In Control

If you read the sidebar I wrote back in Chapter 2 about Unscrupulous Web Consultants (UWCs, for short), you know that not all Web designers are as honest, objective, and informative as you'd like them to be. In fact, if you're not careful and unknowingly hire a UWC, you might find yourself losing control of your own Web design project.

Here are some things you can do to stay in control. Keep them in mind—even if you think your Web designer is as honest and trustworthy as the day is long.

## Communicating Your Needs & Preferences

Communication is the most important aspect of working with any consultant, including Web designers. It's important to keep the channels of communication flowing in both directions throughout the Web design and creation process. After all, you need to make sure you communicate your needs to the Web designer if you expect him to satisfy them. You also need to let him know how you want things done if you expect him to make you happy.

Here are a few things you can do to keep communication flowing and prevent misunderstandings.

### Put/Get It In Writing

Maybe it's because I'm a writer, but I feel very strongly about putting things in writing. You see, you can't argue print. It either says something or it doesn't.

Don't be afraid to write a memo or send a letter to your Web designer to discuss your take on certain points. You can always refer to that document later—hopefully, to tell the Web designer how well he met your needs.

By the same token, your Web designer should provide you with written confirmation of any changes in your business relationship. This protects him and you from misunderstandings.

### Take a Meeting

Meetings are a great way to interact with your Web designer. The communication flows both ways. You can hear what he says and tell him what you think. You can also have other members of your organization on hand to provide information, answer questions, and brainstorm ideas.

When the meeting is over, however, do yourself a favor and summarize the key points in a memo or note. Then make sure the Web designer gets a copy. This will help ensure that you were both hearing the same thing throughout the meeting.

## Feedback

Whenever you have a particular thought about your Web design project, it's important to share it with your Web designer. Is he working too slowly? Are the colors he's selected too bright? Do you wish your logo were larger? Do you have a better picture of your storefront?

Whatever you're thinking, share it! It will make your work relationship better and help you get what you expect from your Web designer. Just be aware that if you start making a lot of changes to your site once the design process is underway, you may incur additional fees. If things don't seem to be going the right way, discuss it with your Web designer *before* things get out of hand.

## Dealing with Ownership Issues

Who owns your domain name? Your Web site? The answer to both of these questions should be *you*. But if you're not careful, you can lose one or both of them.

### Domain Name

Your domain name is most likely something you paid for. But if you let someone else register it for you, that other person may register himself as the owner.

The domain name registration form asks for information for four different contacts or agents:

○ **REGISTRANT** is the name of the individual or company under which the domain name is registered. This should be you or your company.

○ **ADMINISTRATIVE CONTACT** is the individual who is authorized to make changes to the domain name registration information. This should be you.

○ **BILLING CONTACT** is the individual responsible for paying registration fees. Unfortunately, this should also be you.

- ○ **TECHNICAL CONTACT** is the individual or company who maintains the primary domain name server for the Web site. This should be your ISP.

Make sure that your domain name is registered correctly so that you have complete control over it.

**TIP ▶** *You can check to see how your domain name is registered by using the WHOIS Lookup feature on the Network Solutions Web site (http://www.networksolutions.com/). Click the WHOIS Lookup link on the Home page, then enter your domain name in the Search WHOIS form that appears and click Search. Figure 9.2 shows the registration information for one of my sites, wickenburg-az.com.*

### Web Site

When a Web designer builds a Web site for you, he's creating an intellectual property that is protected by copyright law. Did you know that?

Your agreement with the Web designer should include some provision that clearly states who owns copyright to the com-

### Domain Name Kidnapping

Here's my favorite horror story, because I've seen it happen so many times.

A small business owner hires a Web designer to set up a Web site for him. As part of the service the Web designer provides, he registers the company's domain name. But when he fills out the registration form, he enters himself as the Administrative contact and puts his ISP buddy down as the Technical contact. Since these two contacts control the administrative and technical aspects of the registration information, they control the information about where the Web site resides. The small business owner is forced to use the ISP for domain name hosting.

This happened to one of my clients. He was in a hurry to register his domain name and didn't know how to do it himself. He saw an ad in the newspaper for domain name registration and paid $150 to have his domain name registered by an ISP. The ISP set himself up as both Administrative and Technical contacts. When it came time to move his site to my server, the ISP refused to change the server information for the site. There was nothing my client or I could do. It wasn't until several months went by and we threatened legal action that the information was changed. The Administrative contact information was also changed so my client finally has control of his domain name.

pleted site. Make sure it's you. Don't accept anything less. The project should be handled as a "work for hire."

Why? Well suppose you and your Web designer have a falling out—*after* you've already paid him for his work. If he owns the Web site, he could force you to take it offline. Although you'd probably have a good legal case to get the site back, do you really want to deal with lawyers and courts and legal fees?

FIGURE 9.2
You can use the WHOIS Lookup feature on Network Solutions' Web site to see how your domain name (or anyone else's, for that matter) is registered.

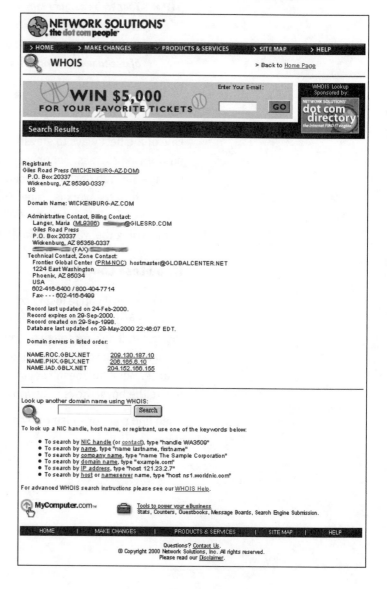

In addition, your Web designer may include copyright notices on each page of the Web site. If so, it should indicate you or your organization as the copyright holder. I recently saw a Web design contract that clearly stated that the client owned copyright to the site. Yet on every page, the Web designer's company appeared as copyright owner. That's not right.

**TIP ▶** *Your Web designer might want to include links to his Web site or an advertisement for his services on your site. Don't allow it. A link or ad for your Web designer does not add anything of use to your customers or clients.*

### Reviewing Work in Progress

One of the best ways to stay in control of a project is to review all work in progress. Set up weekly status meetings or arrange to have the Web designer upload the site to a test server so you can see how the work is going. Then, when you see something you like or don't like, tell the Web designer. This will help keep things going the way you want them to.

### If You Lose Control

If you feel as if you're losing control—things just aren't going the way you expected them to—meet with the Web designer to discuss it. If he's receptive to your comments and seems willing to make changes to get things back on track, give him another chance. But if he doesn't seem interested in recognizing that you're the boss, prove it by firing him.

Then find someone else who can do the job the way you want it done.

# Food for Thought

Ready to hire and work with a Web designer? Stop a moment and think about some of the things this chapter covered. Use the following suggestions to get started. If you want to see what others have to say or want to share your thoughts with other readers, visit the book's companion Web site at **http://www.smallbusinessonweb.com/**.

○ Consult my list of resources for finding a Web designer at the beginning of this chapter. Put them in the order you think is most useful. Did I leave any out?

○ What do you think are the most important qualifications of a Web designer?

○ If you already have a domain name, use WHOIS Lookup to see how it is registered. Are you the Administrative contact? If not, who is? (Take my advice and get it changed to you as soon as possible.)

# PART III

# Going Online

Your Web site has been built and it's exactly what you want to present to the world. Now what do you do?

This part of the book explains how to upload your site to the Web server—the last step to getting it online if you built it yourself or if your Web designer didn't upload it for you. It also tells you how to take advantage of search engines and other techniques to increase your site's exposure. Finally, it covers the things you need to do to update, monitor, and maintain your site.

# Part III Table of Contents

**CHAPTER TEN**

# Uploading Your Site

The last step to getting a Web site online is to put a copy of it on the Web server. This is something you'll have to do if you used the do-it-yourself approach or if your Web designer did not upload the site for you.

This chapter explains how to upload your site to the Web server using FTP. It also explains how to update the pages on the Web server when you make changes to the local copy of your site.

## In This Chapter

ALL ABOUT FTP

UPLOADING & UPDATING YOUR SITE

# All about FTP

I've mentioned FTP a few times in this book. (I even defined it back in Chapter 1.) But now it's time to discuss it in detail, since it's the tool most often used to upload Web sites to a Web server.

## What Is FTP?

FTP stands for *File Transfer Protocol*. It's the standard method of uploading and downloading files on the Internet and it has been around longer than the World Wide Web.

## How FTP Works

In most cases, the computer that is running your Web server software is also running FTP server software. That makes it a Web server and an FTP server at the same time.

FTP client software can "look" into directories accessible on an FTP server. Depending on how access is set up, you may be able to use your FTP client software to download (or *get*) files from the server, upload (or *put*) files to the server, add directories (or folders) on the server, and delete files or directories on the server.

## Security

The system administrator or Webmaster can control access to the directories on the Web server's hard disk with security features built into the FTP server software. If set up properly, these access features can prevent unauthorized individuals from deleting or overwriting important files. They can also prevent unauthorized individuals from accessing files they have no reason to see.

If your Web site resides on your ISPs server, for example, your ISP will limit your access to the directory in which your site resides. You'll have complete control over the contents of that directory. But even if you can see the contents of other directories, you probably won't be able to access individual files or folders within them. Likewise, the owners of other Web sites on the server won't be able to access your Web site's files.

## FTP Software

By FTP software, I mean client software. Unless you're running the Web server yourself, you don't have to worry about FTP server software.

Here's a closer look at your FTP software options.

### Command Line Interface

In the old days, you used FTP by typing commands into a communications software package, such as HyperTerm for Windows or ZTerm for Mac OS. It wasn't fun. The commands were not intuitive and, in many cases, the system you were accessing was Unix based, so you had to know some Unix, too. (I still have a Unix book on my shelf just in case I need to access a Unix system. I hope I never have to open that book again.)

You can still use this method if you can connect to the FTP server with telecommunications software. I don't recommend it. There are better ways. Read on.

### Graphic User Interface

Nowadays, FTP software on Windows and Mac OS is far more intuitive, utilizing a graphic user interface. Click, drag, double-click, use menus. It all works the way you expect it to.

Here are two of my favorite FTP clients:

○ **FTP EXPLORER**, a Windows-based FTP client software package, uses a Windows Explorer-like interface for working with the contents of directories on an FTP server (see Figure 10.1). What's kind of cool about this program, is that the bottom half of the window shows the FTP commands the program sends, as well as the server's responses. You don't have to type any of this information; the software does it for you. Just work with window contents as if you're working with Windows Explorer: to download items, drag them from the FTP Explorer window to a Windows Explorer window; to upload items, drag them from the Windows Explorer window to an FTP Explorer window.

○ **NETFINDER**, a Mac OS-based FTP client software package, uses a Finder-like interface for working with the contents of directories on an FTP server (see Figure 10.2). (You can also open a Transcript window to see the FTP commands NetFinder entered for you.) Use NetFinder's windows as if they were regular Finder windows; drag and drop to download and upload files.

**FIGURE 10.1**
FTP Explorer is a Windows-based FTP client software package.

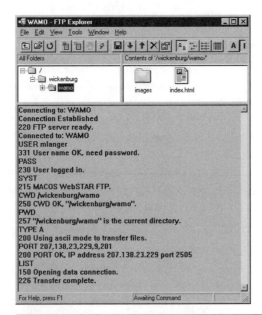

**FIGURE 10.2**
NetFinder is a Mac OS-based FTP client software package.

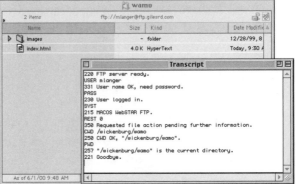

**TIP ▶**  *You can download these and other FTP software programs—*
*including Fetch, a popular Mac OS program—on CNET*
*Download.com, http://www.download.com/.*

### FTP Capabilities of Web Authoring Software

Most of the Web authoring programs I discussed in Chapter 8 have built-in FTP capabilities. These are usually very limited, allowing you to simply upload files to the Web server.

PageMill's FTP features are a good example. When you build a Web site, you can specify FTP options that identify the FTP server name, the site's folder on the server, and your login information (see Figure 10.3). Then you can select one or more files or folders in PageMill's Site Details window (see Figure 10.4), and

**FIGURE 10.3**
You can specify a Web site's FTP settings within PageMill.

**FIGURE 10.4**
When you select a file or folder within the Site Details window, uploading it to the Web server is as simple as clicking a button or choosing a command.

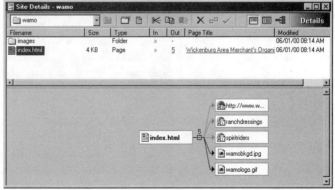

use an Upload button or command to upload them to the Web server.

But some programs, such as Dreamweaver, have very powerful FTP capabilities. Once you specify FTP settings, you can connect to the FTP server and view the contents of both your remote and local site folders, right in the Site window (see Figure 10.5). To download a file from the remote folder to the local folder, select it and click the Get button. To upload a file from the local folder to the remote folder, select it and click the Put button. Both windows are automatically updated whenever you make a change.

**FIGURE 10.5**
Dreamweaver gives you access to both Put and Get commands so you can transfer files both to and from the server.

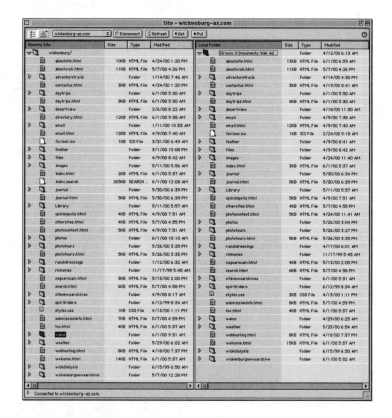

# Uploading & Updating Your Site

Now that you know about FTP and how it works, let's take a look at how you can use FTP to upload and update your Web site.

### Local & Remote Folders, Revisited

Back in Chapter 8, I discussed the concept of having a local and remote Web site folder. The local folder is the folder on your hard disk that contains your entire Web site. You should have built the folder hierarchy before you started saving pages and storing resources. This way, all the references to resources and links to other site pages remain intact. You should also have tested all of your pages to make sure they appear the way you intended, with no missing resources or broken links.

When you upload your site to the remote folder, you're copying the contents of the local folder into the remote folder. When you're finished, you could open the remote folder and see the same files in the same file hierarchy as in the local folder. (Figure 10.5 shows an example of the two folders, side by side, within Dreamweaver. You may notice that the remote folder has a few extra files; these are files created by the Web server software that are not needed locally.)

*Don't copy the local folder into the remote folder. Copy the* contents *of the local folder into the remote folder.*

### How To Do It

The method you select to perform the upload will vary based on the FTP software you use.

### Using Built-In FTP

If you're using the built-in FTP capabilities of your Web authoring tool—the method I recommend—follow the instructions in the software manual to specify your FTP settings, including the FTP server name, directory (or path), user ID, and password. You should get all of this information from your ISP or System administrator. Then select either the site's root folder or the contents of the site's root folder and use the appropriate Upload or Put command within the software to upload the entire site. If you correctly set up the server and directory information for your site, the files will be properly uploaded into the remote folder.

### Using Graphic User Interface FTP Software

If you're using a graphic user interface FTP client software package such as FTP Explorer or NetFinder, connect to the FTP server using the information you get from your ISP or System administrator: FTP server name, directory, user ID, and password.

Next, open the remote folder so you can see its contents—it should be empty (or almost empty) if you haven't uploaded your site yet. In Windows Explorer or the Mac OS Finder, open the local folder so you can see its contents.

Now select all of the contents of the local folder and drag it into the window for the remote folder. The download should begin. If it doesn't, check the manual that came with the software; the instructions may differ from these.

### Using Command Line Interface FTP Software

If you're using a command line interface, you must be an FTP expert and you don't need my help. (If you do need my help, take my advice and don't use the command line interface!)

### The First Time

The first time you upload your site to the Web server, all the files you add should be brand new to the server. You won't be overwriting anything—except maybe a default Home page the ISP put there for you.

You should be able to check the upload right away. Fire up your Web browser and enter the URL for your Web site. Your Home page should appear. If it doesn't, either you incorrectly named your Home page or something went wrong during the upload.

Check the instructions your ISP or system administrator provided for assistance. If that doesn't help, call their technical support staff.

### Updating Your Pages

Now, every time you make a change to any of the pages or resources on your site, you'll make those changes on the local copy of the Web site—not the remote copy. The only way to get those changes onto the Web server so everyone can see them is to re-upload the page or resource.

Updating Web site files works the same way as uploading them for the first time. There are only two differences:

○ You don't have to upload all the files for the site. Just the ones that have changed.

○ Because the files already exist on the server, you will overwrite them with new versions.

Follow the instructions earlier in this chapter to upload the changed files. Select only those files that have changed. This will save time, especially if your connection to the Internet is at slower modem speeds.

*Although you can update your Web site by re-uploading all pages, it's only necessary to upload the pages that have changed.*

# Food for Thought

This chapter provided some straightforward instructions for getting your Web site onto the Web server. Here are a few things you can do to prepare for the big day when you go online.

If you'd like to share some thoughts about FTP with other readers, visit the book's companion Web site at **http://www.smallbusinessonweb.com/**.

○ Consider your Web authoring program. Does it have built-in FTP capabilities? Check the manual to find out.

○ Gather together the information you need to access your Web site via FTP: the FTP server or host, directory, user ID, and password.

○ Visit CNET Download.com at **http://www.download.com/** and select one or more FTP client software packages for your computer platform. Experiment with them to see which one you like best.

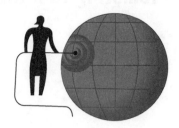

## CHAPTER ELEVEN

# Directing Visitors to Your Site

Once your site is up and running, don't just sit back and wait for hits. Guide customers or clients to your Home page. In this chapter, I explain how, by using materials you probably already have and by taking advantage of one of the Web's most used (and misunderstood) features: search engines.

## In This Chapter

PROMOTING YOUR SITE

GETTING FOUND

# Promoting Your Site

One of the simplest and most cost effective ways to promote your Web site to the people who will be most interested in its contents is through the use of materials you probably already have. Here's a quick look at the documents you can use as Web site promotion tools.

*Don't throw away existing printed materials that don't include your Web site's URL. But make sure all newly printed materials include this important piece of contact information.*

### Letterhead & Envelopes

Almost every company I know, regardless of size, uses pre-printed letterhead and envelopes for written correspondence. But who says the printing can't include your Web site's URL and e-mail addresses?

By including this information on your letterhead and envelopes, you're announcing the address for a virtual location of your business. And it shouldn't cost a penny more.

### Business Cards

Business cards are probably the most cost effective communication tool around. This tiny card can fit a wealth of information on it—and be carried around in a pocket.

Your company's URL should appear on every business card you print for owners, managers, and other employees.

### Forms

Does your company use preprinted forms, such as estimates, invoices, and packing slips? How about including your Web site's URL on them as well? It's just another way to spread the word.

## Brochures & Catalogs

Brochures and catalogs are another important place you should include your Web site's URL—especially if your Web site includes a catalog or online shopping feature. These documents usually go to the people who are most interested in your business as customers or clients. Letting them know you have a Web site can give them another way to learn more about your products and services.

**TIP ▶** *Some companies with Web sites that offer online shopping offer special discounts to customers who order via the Web. This not only promotes the site, but it encourages customers to take advantage of a more cost effective ordering method. The more people you can get to use online catalogs and ordering, the fewer printed catalogs and telephone order takers you'll have to provide.*

## Print Ads

One of my clients has had a Web site for the past six months. He runs ads in the local newspaper every single week. Do you think he'd include his Web site's URL in the ad? He doesn't, but he should!

Again, what's the extra cost of including that one additional piece of information where people could see it? Nothing! (Or pretty darn close to nothing!) The same goes for Yellow Pages ads and television commercials.

**TIP ▶** *I don't recommend including your URL in a radio commercial if it must be spelled out. For example, one of my companies, Giles Road Press, has the ridiculous domain name of gilesrd.com. (What was I thinking?) Every time I give someone the URL, I have to spell it out. Can you imagine that on a radio commercial?*

### E-Mail Signatures

Most e-mail programs support the inclusion of a custom **SIGNATURE** at the bottom of each e-mail message you send. You should already be using this e-mail feature to include your name and contact information. But you should also be using it to promote your Web site by including its complete URL in the signature. This is a great, free way to spread the word to people who probably already have Internet access.

# Getting Found

Web surfers who know about your organization, products, or services but don't have your URL may rely on search engines and directories to find your Web site. Still others, who don't even know your company exists, may use **SEARCH ENGINES** to enter search phrases that should apply to you. How do you increase the odds of having your site listed among those found?

This part of the chapter explains how search engines work and tells you what you can do to get your Web site found by the people searching for it.

**TIP ▶** *Search Engine Watch is an excellent resource for getting more information about search engines—including lists of search engines. Visit it at http://www.searchenginewatch.com/.*

### Search Engine Basics

Search engines are one of the most misunderstood features of the Web. Few people know how they work or why different search engines come up with different results for the same

**SIGNATURE**
Text that can appear at the end of every outgoing e-mail message.

**SEARCH ENGINE**
An online utility that enables Web surfers to find Web sites based on search criteria they provide.

search phrases. Even fewer people know how the search engines know about all the Web sites they list on the search results pages.

Here's a quick look at how search engines work.

**TIP ▶** *To learn more about how to use search engines to find Web sites, check out* **Search Engines for the World Wide Web: Visual QuickStart Guide,** *a Peachpit Press book by Alfred and Emily Glossbrenner. You can learn more about it at http://www.peachpit.com/books/catalog/K5842.html.*

### Robots and Spiders and Crawlers—Oh My!

Many search engines—such as HotBot (http://www.hotbot.com/) and WebCrawler (http://www.webcrawler.com/)—utilize software programs called *robots*, *spiders*, or c*rawlers*. These programs

**Newbie Search Confusion**

I know how to use a search engine and I assumed that everyone else did. That is, until recently. I began talking to Web newbies and watching them access the Internet. Here are some of the startling things I learned:

○ Some people think the only way to access a Web page is by clicking a link on another page. If the site they want to access is not linked through the default Home page that appears in their Web browser—normally a portal site like Yahoo!, MSN, or NetCenter—they can't access the site.

○ Some people think you search for a site by entering its URL or domain name in a search box and clicking Search or Go or whatever. Unfortunately, if the site has not been indexed or listed in that search engine's database, the site will not appear in the list of search results.

○ Some people do not understand that search results seldom fit on one page. They look no further than the first page of results to find sites they seek.

○ Some people think that the featured sites that appear in search results lists are featured because they're the best match for their criteria. They don't realize that many of those sites paid to be featured and may not even be good matches for their criteria.

○ Some AOL users think that if a Web site does not have an AOL keyword, they cannot access it via AOL. (Other AOL users don't understand that you don't need AOL to access the Web, but that's another sad yet unrelated problem.)

These examples illustrate how difficult it can be to get your site found by newcomers to the Web. But until these people become more search savvy, there isn't much you can do.

venture out onto the Web when activity is low (whenever t*hat is*) and search for new pages. When they find a site they've never visited before, they follow all the internal links within the pages to learn about the pages on the site. They also occasionally (but not often enough) revisit sites to update the information they already have.

What kind of information do they gather? Well, that depends on the program. Some programs gather just Web page titles—the information that appears in the Web browser title bar. (This is not the same as a file name). Others gather every single word in the page. Still others gather information stored in special meta tags embedded in the page (more on that later).

### Directories

While some search engines depend solely on robots, spiders, and crawlers, others—such as Excite (**http://www.excite.com/**) and Yahoo! (**http://www.yahoo.com/**)—start with a directory that entries can be manually added to. Some of these directories are static, containing only the information manually entered. Others use directory entries to send out robots, crawlers, and spiders to gather information directly from the Web sites entered.

### The Database

The information gathered about Web sites—whether gathered by robots, etc., or by manual entries into a directory—is stored in a database that can be indexed and searched. Web surfers search the database based on words or phrases. Sites that match the criteria are displayed in a search results list.

*When you use a search engine to find a Web site, you're searching that search engine's database of sites, not the Web itself.*

### Who's On First

Search engine result lists are usually very long—sometimes with tens of thousands of matches. (Of course, not all of them appear on one page; you'll have to click through hundreds of pages to see them all.) The sites that most closely match the search word or phrase should appear at the top...right? Well, sometimes. It depends on the search engine and what you entered.

Figure 11.1 shows the first page of results for a query on Search.com (http://www.search.com/) for horse *camping in arizona*. (I'm going camping tomorrow and it's on my mind.) If you can read the tiny print, you can see that not all of the pages seem to relate to the search phrase. (If you can't read the tiny print, please take my word for it.) Yet several pages further into the search results is information about the campground I'll be going to. Why didn't it come up on top?

The answer is: it depends. Most search engines list results based on how well the search word or phrase was matched in its database. (In my opinion, this is the way it s*hould work*.) Others—such as Direct Hit (http://www.directhit.com/)—list results based on popularity—how many people click through to that page. Still others put paid-for listings near the top and others below it.

And of course, whether a listing appears at all depends on whether the listing was added to the search engine's database to begin with.

### The Bottom Line

The bottom line is this: to be found by a search engine, your site must be included in that search engine's database. Your job is to get included in as many search engine databases and directories as possible.

**TIP ▶** *Search Engine Watch's Search Engine Submission Tips page (see Figure 11.2; http://www.searchenginewatch.com/ webmasters/) is a great place to learn more about how search engines work and how you can increase your odds of being near the top of the search results list.*

**FIGURE 11.1**
The first search results page for a
search.com search.

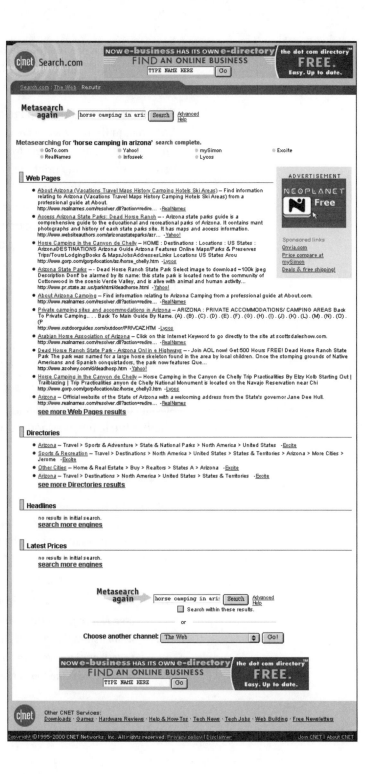

FIGURE 11.2

The Search Engine Submission Tips page on Search Engine Watch is a great way to learn more about getting your site found by search engines.

## Search Engine Submission Tips

This section of Search Engine Watch (formerly called A Webmaster's Guide To Search Engines) is primarily for webmasters, site owners and web marketers. It covers search engine submission and registration issues. It explains how search engines find and rank web pages, with an emphasis on what webmasters can do to improve their search engine placement by using better page design, HTML meta tags, and other tips.

"Site subscribers" have access to even more in-depth information about submission issues and get extra benefits. Click here to learn more about becoming a site subscriber

If this is a first time visit, read the following pages in order, to learn about the basics of search engine design. The navigation box at the bottom of each page will allow you to easily load the next one.

**Important To Read**

- Introduction to Search Engine Design
- Major Search Engines
- How Search Engines Work
- How Search Engines Rank Web Pages
- Search Engine Features For Webmasters
- Search Engine Design Tips
- How To Use Meta Tags
- Search Engine Report Mailing List

**Optional But Helpful**

- Coping With Frames
- Checking Your URL
- Search Engine Display Chart
- SpiderSpotting
- SpiderSpotting Chart
- Measuring Link Popularity
- Search Engines And Capitalization
- What Is A Bridge or Doorway Page?
- How Search Engines Regionalize
- Yahoo Special Report

**Additional Topics Of Interest**

- Search Engine Software For Your Web Site
  This page covers ways to add a search engine to your web site, one of the site's most frequently asked questions.
- Search Engine Design Resources
- Search Engine Technology Resources
- How Big Are Search Engines?

Remember to keep up with search engine developments by subscribing to the free Search Engine Report newsletter, a monthly recap of the latest search engine happenings.

Even better, consider becoming a Search Engine Watch site subscriber. You'll get access to additional material about search engine submission issues and other benefits.

| Choose Another Page | ⬍ | Go |

or use the site map if you can't run JavaScript.
You may also search the site.

**Free Newsletter!**
Enter your email address below to get a monthly newsletter about search engines

Subscribe

Learn more about the newsletter

Submit your site properly the first time - Learn the tips on how submitting should be done. Avoid making the mistakes that so many other Webmasters make daily!

Like This Site? Click Here To Tell A Friend!

By Danny Sullivan
Search Engine Watch
http://searchenginewatch.com/
Copyright © 1996-2000 internet.com Corp.
http://www.internet.com

## Using Meta Tags

If you were reading carefully, you probably caught my use of the phrase **META TAG**. I didn't define it then because I was saving it for now.

### Meta Tags, Defined

Meta tags are HTML tags that can be inserted in the HEAD part of an HTML document to embed document information. Now, in English: meta tags enable you to include information about a Web page where it won't be seen by site visitors but can be seen by robots, spiders, and crawlers.

There are many uses for meta tags, but the ones you should be most interested in are for storing description and keyword information. This is the information most often picked up by robots, etc.

**TIP ▶** *Be sure to include the description and keyword meta tags in all the pages of your Web site. Remember, not everyone visits your site starting with the Home page.*

### Description

The description information should be a short, concise description of the site or page. Don't repeat the page title; it's a waste of words. Since you're usually limited to 256 characters, make the most of them.

The format for the description meta tag is as follows:

<META name="description" content="*concise description of Web site or page*">

What does the description meta tag look like in an HTML document? Figure 11.3 shows an example from the Home page of one of my sites, wickenburg-az.com (http://www.wickenburg-az.com/).

### Keywords

The keyword information should be a list of key words or phrases, separated by commas. Again, there's usually a limit of

256 characters for keywords, but not all robots, etc., accept that many. If a robot, etc., is limited to, say, 150 characters, it will take the first 150 characters it finds. For that reason, you should put the most important keywords at the beginning of the meta tag. Also, don't repeat the same words over and over again because most robots, etc., are programmed to ignore repetition—and a few will actually penalize you for it!

The format for the keyword meta tag is as follows:

<META name="keywords" content="*list of key words and phrases separated by commas*">

Figure 11.3 also shows the keywords tag from the Home page of wickenburg-az.com. Note that it includes the words that best describe the site's contents—and even some misspellings of those words! (When I analyze my site's logs, I often find that site visitors used an incorrect spelling of Wickenburg and still find my site.)

```
<HEAD>

<TITLE>wickenburg-az.com, Virtual Community of Wickenburg, AZ</TITLE>

<META NAME="description" CONTENT="The virtual community of Wickenburg, AZ. We're putting
Wickenburg online!">

<META NAME="keywords" CONTENT="Wickenburg, Wickinberg, Wickenberg, Arizona, AZ, Wickenburg
AZ, virtual community, real estate, gold mine, mining, gold, history, horse, ranching,
Hassayampa, retirement, old west, dude ranch">

</HEAD>
```

## Meta Tags in Search Results

Figure 11.4 shows a close-up of some search results for the phrase *horse camping*.

Most of the entries include the name of the page, followed by a brief description. The description comes from the description meta tag. This is how you want your pages to appear in search engine results.

META TAG
An HTML tag for embedding certain types of information in a Web page document.

But look at the second entry, "Camping at Crazy Horse." The description text doesn't appear to be a description at all. Sure enough, when you click the link you can see that the "description" is really the first handful of words from the Home page (see Figure 11.5).

Now look at the last entry in the Figure. This entry is a real mess. It appears that the Web author included keywords in the page's title, as well as the description. Figures 11.6 and 11.7 partially confirm this; the title is entered three times in the HTML document's source code. Although the description meta tag appears okay, the error in the title's code may have caused the robot, etc., to pull up the wrong information for the description.

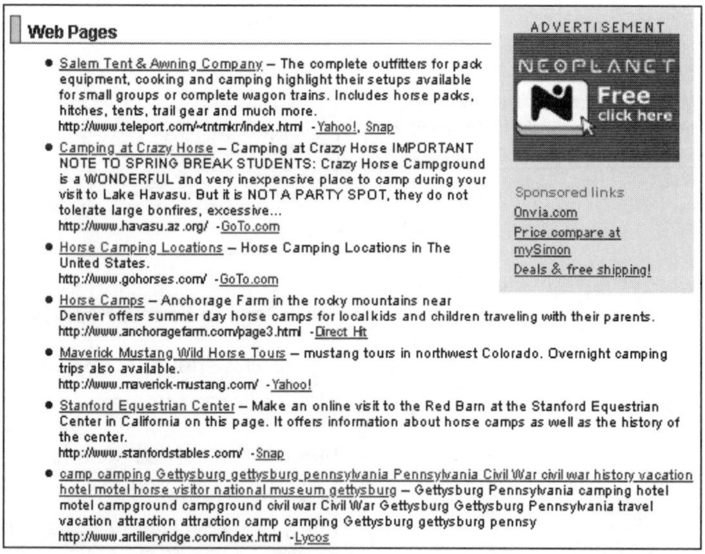

**FIGURE 11.4**
A close-up of some search results reveals how meta tags are not always properly used.

**FIGURE 11.5**
When you omit the description meta tag from an HTML document, the first handful of words on the page appear as a description.

As you can see, when you set up meta tags correctly, your site's listing in search engines that use meta tags can be exactly what you want it to be. But when you do it wrong, the listing is wrong.

## Adding Your Site to Search Engine Databases

Once you've set up meta tags for all the pages on your site, you can help improve the chances of robots, etc. finding your site by manually adding your site's information to search engine directories. Then, if that search engine sends out robots, etc., your site will be found and indexed.

**FIGURE 11.6**
In this example, the page title includes keywords,...

**FIGURE 11.7**
...a fact that's confirmed when you inspect the page's source code. Perhaps the inclusion of the title code in triplicate is what messed up this page's listing in the search results; the description meta tag appears okay.

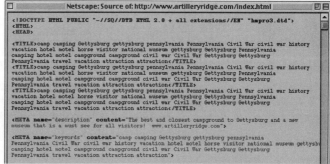

## Hiding a Page with Meta Tags

There may be instances when you don't want a particular page on your site indexed by a robot, etc. For example, perhaps a page is private, for the use of a few people who have the exact URL of the page. Having the page listed in search engine results lists won't keep it private for long.

You can use a meta tag to block robots, etc., from indexing it:

```
<META name="robots" content="noindex">
```

This really works. My Web server sits on a computer desk beside my main production computer. Sometimes I leave the monitor turned on so I can watch activity. (You think I'd have better things to do with my time, right?) I've noticed that within 10 seconds of adding one of my sites to a directory, a robot sometimes appears on my server to check out the site's Home page. Now that's service!

To add your site to a search engine's directory, begin by visiting that search engine's main page. Now look for a link that says something like "Add a site" or "Add a URL" or "Suggest a Site." This link is usually in very small letters near the top or bottom of the Home page, but sometimes it can be buried on other pages. And sometimes it may not appear at all. Figure 11.8 shows how it appears at the bottom of the Excite Home page (**http:// www.excite.com/**).

*Unfortunately, you can't add your Web site to every search engine. Some search engines let their robots, etc., do all the work on their own. Others are very particular about which sites they include.*

When you click the link, a page with instructions for adding your site will appear. Read the information and follow the instructions. Figure 11.9 shows Excite's Add URL page. It offers a pretty straightforward form. Fill it out and click the Send button. That's all there is to it.

In some cases, a message will appear with some kind of confirmation that your request is being processed. Sometimes you'll be told that it takes four to eight weeks (or some other silly

**FIGURE 11.8**
You can find a tiny link for adding a URL at the bottom of Excite's Home page.

period) to process your request. You might want to make a note of it, then try the search engine after a reasonable amount of time has passed. If you're not listed, try adding it again.

FIGURE 11.9
This page on Excite offers a simple form for adding your site to its database of Web sites.

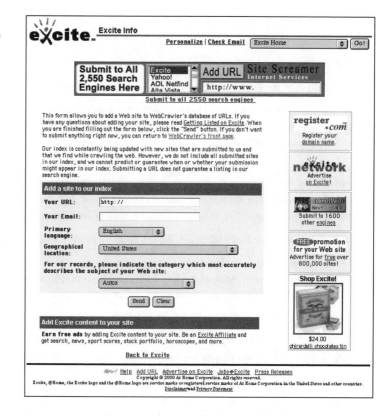

## Submit to All 2,550 Search Engines Here

Sound familiar? It should—it's on a banner in the screen shot in Figure 11.9. It'll also come to you in junk e-mail and flash at you periodically as you surf the Web.

Beware of services that claim to submit information about your Web site to hundreds or thousands of search engines all at once. I've tried these services and found two things:

- They seldom work as advertised. In fact, I've found that my site was not added to listings that it was supposed to be added to.

- They often require a fee for listing your site with more than a handful of search engines.

My advice: if you have the time to try one of these services, go right ahead. Just don't expect them to work. And don't pay for the service.

## Adding Your Site to Directories & Other Sites

You can also add your site as a link to other sites, including directories of sites in your geographical or business area. This is especially useful if the other site is a good match for yours. For example, a state directory of accountants would be a good

### Paying for Links

I do not believe in paying for links. There. I said it. Now let me explain.

There are two ways to make money with a Web site: sell a darn good product or service that people are willing to buy online or sell advertising space on the site. Many Web sites exist solely to make money using the second method—selling advertising space to other Web sites.

Some of these Web sites are portals for Web surfers to access other sites. They often call themselves *directories* and they offer categorized or searchable links to other sites. The sites that are listed are the ones that have paid a fee. Or perhaps any site can be listed, but the ones that pay a fee are listed first or with a banner ad. The point is, the site's links exist to generate revenue for the site.

Is the person paying for that listing getting his money's worth? Well, it depends on many things:

○ Is the directory site popular? If the site doesn't get many hits, few people will see its links. This is the biggest problem with many of the pay directory sites: they're more interested in collecting link fees than promoting their own site. Would you advertise in a newspaper that didn't have a good circulation?

○ Is the directory site related to the site that's advertising on it? If the directory specializes in real estate, for example, it won't do much to promote the sites of unrelated businesses.

○ Do people come to the directory site for links or for some other content? If they're coming for other content and they're like me, they'll ignore the ads and most of the links.

○ Are the other links for quality sites? When I go to a directory Web site and half the links are worthless, I'll move on to another site before I waste any more of my time.

Here's a true story. I know a certain Chamber of Commerce that charges its members $70 a year to include a link on the Chamber's Web site. (That's paying members, mind you, paying even more for this link.) When asked why there's a fee, the Webmaster claimed that the money collected paid to link the Chamber's site to other sites, most of which were state and tourism related. Can someone explain to me how the local appliance fix-it guy would benefit from having his site indirectly linked to a state tourism site?

I will agree that there *are* some instances when paying for a link to another site can really get you more hits—hits that are valuable to your business. But like any other advertising expenditure, you should carefully consider what you're getting for your money before you pay. Then monitor hits from that site to see if you're getting what you paid for.

Finally, I believe that if your site is included in as many free search engine databases and directories as possible, and referenced in all your printed materials, you'll get all the hits you need...and then some.

match for a CPA and a tourism directory would be a good match for a hotel or tour service.

To add yourself to one of these directories, begin by visiting the site. Make sure it's a good match for you business. Then poke around until you see some way to add a link or ask about adding a link. If all else fails, e-mail the Webmaster.

Be aware that some sites charge a fee for links. Keep your advertising budget in mind when considering whether a link is worth the fee. (And please read the sidebar on the next page for my very strong opinions on the subject.)

Other sites will only ask for a reciprocating link. Before agreeing to that, make sure the site is up to your standards. I discuss reciprocating links in more detail back in Chapter 6.

# Food for Thought

By now, you should have a good idea of how you can promote your Web site. Here are a few suggestions for putting those ideas into action. To share your thoughts with other readers or see what other readers had to say about the topics in this chapter, visit the book's companion Web site, **http://www.smallbusinessonweb.com/**.

○   Think about the printed materials you use in your business. Which ones can be used to promote your Web site?

○   Make a list of the ten search engines you use most. (If you don't know ten search engines, visit Search Engine Watch at **http://www.searchenginewatch.com/** to find them.) Now use those search engines to look for companies like yours. What do you think of the search results?

○   Write down the description and keywords that apply to your site as a whole. Use them in meta tags on your Home page. Now add appropriate description and keyword meta tags to the rest of the pages on your site.

o   Visit the ten search engines you listed a moment ago. Look for and follow "Add URL" links on each site to add your Web site to the search engine's database.

o   Use your favorite search engines to look for sites that would be appropriate for reciprocating links. Request links and see how you do.

# CHAPTER TWELVE

# Maintaining Your Site

The Web publishing process never ends. Once you create a Web site and put it online, you're responsible for keeping it up to date. That means adding content and features so repeat visitors always find something new and interesting. While you're at it, you'll want to monitor your site usage logs to keep track of page hits and referrers. This chapter covers all areas of maintaining a Web site, including what you should look for in Web access logs.

## In This Chapter

Updating Site Content & Features

Monitoring Usage

# Updating Site Content & Features

Throughout this book, I've stressed the importance of keeping your Web site up-to-date and interesting. Let me take a few moments to explain exactly what I mean and what you should be doing.

## Keeping Content Fresh

I'm sure this has happened to you: You visit a Web site and see some kind of bold or flashing announcement about a new product or special price. Interested, you follow appropriate links to learn more. Then you learn—from a page copyright date or "last updated" date—that the page hasn't been updated in six months. Or two years.

This has happened to me more times than I can count. It's annoying, because I feel as if I were conned into following up on something that may or may not still be valid. It also makes me wonder just how up-to-date the rest of the site is. And whether the company cares about it. Or even whether the company is still in business.

If your Web site contains any time-sensitive material, it's *vital* that you update it on a regular basis. Old news is bad news. And bad news is bad for business.

## Adding New Content

Once your site is up and running and all the bugs have been worked out, you might want to consider adding new content. This can increase the site's usefulness to visitors. It will also show repeat visitors that the site is always evolving and getting better.

For example, suppose in your rush to get your site online, you decided not to include some of the technical support information your company had accumulated. Just because you didn't include it when the site first went live doesn't mean you can't include it later. Create Web pages with the information, link them into your existing pages, and upload them to the site.

Or perhaps you've found that a large percentage of your telephone inquiries are from people who want to know where they can find your product locally. Add a list of authorized resellers to your Web site. This can cut down the number of inquiries for this information. Your customers with access to the Web can get the information they need quickly, without a [long distance] telephone call and you won't need as many people to answer the phones.

## Adding New Features

Likewise, you can also add new features. This can make the site more useful for both you and your site's visitors.

For example, say your site includes an e-mail link for sales queries. Site visitors are using this link to send e-mail to your sales department, but half the customers fail to mention what product they're interested in and a quarter of them fail to include a phone number. If you can process CGIs on your Web server, you can solve the problem by removing the e-mail link and adding an e-mail form that includes fields for the information you need. This makes it impossible for the visitor to omit necessary information.

Or perhaps you've found that a high percentage of support calls ask the same few questions. You can add a searchable database of frequently asked questions or support documents. You can also add a form that visitors can use to ask technical support questions, thus adding them to the database. This can benefit customers who need help when your business is closed and can reduce your support costs.

## Test, Test, Test!

I can't bug you enough about testing your site for problems or errors. (At least that's what my editor says; she keeps reminding me to bug you.)

Let's face it, when your Web site has problems, you have problems. Whether it's a missing graphic or a broken link, if a visitor sees it, he's going to wonder just how much you care about your Web site. Then he's going to wonder if you put the same care into your product or service. That's not good for you.

Testing is part of maintaining a Web site two ways:

○ When you make changes to your site, test every page to make sure that the changes did not negatively effect their appearance or links.

○ Periodically, test all pages—especially external links on pages—to make sure they appear and work properly.

*You have no control over external links; if a page you linked to disappears from the Web, the only way you'll learn about the resulting bad link is if you try it. Be sure to fix or remove any bad links you find.*

# Monitoring Usage

Once your site is up and running, it should start getting hits. At least you hope so. But how can you tell for sure? And what can you learn about the people who visit your site?

The answer is in the Web server logs for your site.

### Log Analysis Software

Did you ever look at a Web log? Figure 12.1 shows part of a log from my server, which runs WebSTAR software. As you can see, it isn't exactly the easiest thing to decipher. And this particular log, which is for the month of May 2000, is over 26 MB in size!

Log analysis software can help. This software can take raw Web server log files and make sense of them by summarizing information in a format you can use.

## Finding a Program

There are many log analysis software products out there. They range in price from free to thousands of dollars. In most cases, you can download a trial version of the software from its developer's Web site and see how you like it before you pay.

Finding Web analysis software isn't difficult. Begin by visiting the Web site for the developer of your Web server. Then follow links for "add-ons" or "utilities." Or just search the site for *log analysis*. You should be able to find some options. Figure 12.2 shows the list available on StarNine's WebSTAR pages (http://www.starnine.com/webstar/).

I tried several programs before settling on Summary Pro by Summary.Net (http://www.summary.net/). It costs $249 and has the features I need to generate reports for all the Web sites on my server. If you have only one site on your server, the basic version of Summary should be all you need; it costs only $59. Summary works with a variety of Web server software packages and is available for both Windows and Mac OS.

## If Your ISP Runs the Server...

If your ISP runs the Web server on which your site resides, he's likely to offer one of three options:

○ **THE ISP MAY GIVE YOU ACCESS TO WEB LOG ANALYSIS SOFTWARE REPORTS FOR YOUR WEB SERVER.** This will utilize the software he's decided to run and may not be customizable. But it's better than

**FIGURE 12.2**
The StarNine Web site lists a number of Web log analysis programs that will work with the WebSTAR Web server software.

**STARNINE**

News · Store · Products · WebSTAR · Support · Search · Site Map · Company Info · Extending WebSTAR

Powered by WEBSTAR SERVER SUITE 4

## Extending WebSTAR: log site analysis: log analysis

**Funnel Web Pro** BundleUP!
Developer: Active Concepts
Developed by Active Concepts, Funnel Web provides fast, flexible processing of a variety of log file formats, and can generate a number of different reports as charts, graphs, text or HTML output. The Pro version supports multi-domain and virtual host reports.

**Funnel Web Standard** BundleUP!
Developer: Active Concepts
Developed by Active Concepts, Funnel Web provides fast, flexible processing of a variety of log file formats, and can generate a number of different reports as charts, graphs, text or HTML output. The Standard version supports log file analysis for single domains or hosts—see Funnel Web Pro for multi-domain and virtual host support.

**LogDoor** BundleUP!
Developer: Open Door Networks
LogDoor is a real-time log analysis tool for use with single or multiple "sites" on your server. LogDoor can produce HTML or text reports of site traffic based on WebSTAR's log file, including reports of error messages.

**Funnel Web Lite** BundleUP!
Developer: Active Concepts
Included with WebSTAR Server Suite 4 Installer (v4.1 or later), Funnel Web Lite provides fast, flexible processing of a variety of log file formats, and can generate a number of different reports as charts, graphs, text or HTML output. Funnel Web Lite is a fully-functional version of Funnel Web Standard edition, limited by volume of 50,000 hits per report.

**Analog**
Developer: Jason T. Linhart
Jason T. Linhart's Macintosh port of a free and very useful log analysis tool. Two Frontier scripts for automating Analog's output, Analogger2 and UpDateWebStats, are available from Three River Internet Software.

**FlashStats**
Developer: Maximized Software
FlashStats, from Maximized Software, can analyze a wide variety of log formats and provides useful reports like Daily Totals, Bad URLs, Search Phrases, Top Referrers, and more; filtering options allow you to concentrate reports on useful data.

**LogTran**
Developer: Summary
LogTran is a shareware utility for Macintosh computers to translate WebSTAR log files into NCSA Combined (Extended) log format. This is useful for getting WebSTAR logs into a format that can be read by log analysis packages that don't directly support WebSTAR formats, such as WebTrends.LogTran can filter out entries based on the hostname, request, agent string or virtual host name.

**Sawmill**
Developer: Flowerfire
Sawmill from Flowerfire is a powerful, hierarchichal log analysis tool that can process numerous kinds of log files. Sawmill allows you to both process logs and view statistics from a web browser, and adds log statistics to a database for maximum speed, efficiency, and flexibility. PowerPC only.

**ServerStat**
Developer: Kitchen Sink Software
This freeware application by Kitchen Sink Software has a number of features for filtering and customizing its WebSTAR log analysis and reports, and analyzes Gopher logs as well. ServerStat can also process multiple log files into a single report.

**Summary**
Developer: Summary.Net
A log analysis tool from Summary.Net, Summary gives you a variety of useful information about the activity on your server, including which search terms were used most often in locating your site or which search robots have accessed your site most frequently. (See also Summary Pro).

**Summary Pro**
Developer: Summary.Net
A log analysis tool from Summary.Net, Summary Pro offers more advanced control over virtual domain reports than the basic Summary product.

**WebStat**
Developer: Phil Harvey
Writen by Phil Harvey this application analyzes your WebSTAR logs and creates reports.

**Wusage**
Developer: Boutell.Com
Wusage from Boutell.Com provides a wide range of information about the traffic on your server, and can generate charts in addition to HTML text in its output.

**WWWStat4Mac**
Developer: Redpoint Software
A shareware log processing utility from Redpoint Software which can handle both WebSTAR and CLF log files.

**HitList**
Developer: Accrue
From Accrue Software, Hit List is a configurable log analysis tool for Windows NT which can handle WebSTAR's CLF or ExLF log output (via an included "Data Collector".)

**WebTrends**
Developer: WebTrends Corp.
Log analysis tool for Windows NT--can generate reports on WebSTAR's log format files by using LogTran (see listing in Extending WebSTAR).

**Didn't find what you were looking for?**

Extending WebSTAR has identified 18 relevant listings outside the current category. Click the button below to view the additional suggestions.

Show Suggestions

Do you want to suggest a product for Extending WebSTAR? Want to update info for an existing entry? Visit the suggestion form...

Home News Store Products WebSTAR Support Search Site Map Company & Contact Info
Extending WebSTAR

nothing. (This is what I do for the folks who maintain Web sites on my server.)

○ **THE ISP MAY ALLOW YOU TO DOWNLOAD YOUR OWN WEB USAGE LOGS.** You can then run Web analysis software on them on your own computer. This gives you more flexibility as far as software is concerned, but downloading logs every time you want to run a report can be a real pain in the butt—especially if your logs are 20 MB or larger in size!

○ **THE ISP MAY NOT GIVE YOU ACCESS TO ANY USAGE STATISTICS AT ALL.** How inconsiderate. Try reasoning with him. If that doesn't work, either live with it or get a new ISP.

### What to Look At

If your Web analysis software is powerful, it will probably offer dozens of reports (see Figure 12.3). You can waste a lot of time trying to make use of them all. Here are the statistics that I find most useful.

FIGURE 12.3
Summary Pro offers dozens of reports—far more than the average Webmaster needs.

# SUMMARY.NET™

The Next Step in Information Technology **REPORT** **MENU** **CONFIG**

## List of Reports
for wickenburg-az.com

| Time | Content | Referrers | Visitors | Browser |
|---|---|---|---|---|
| Hourly Report | Pages | Domains | Root Domains | Browsers |
| Daily Report | Downloads | Referers | Domains | Screen Size |
| Weekly Report | Graphics | Search Words | Hosts | Color Depth |
| Monthly Report | Others | Search Phrases | Known Robots | Window Width |
| Yearly Report | All Requests | Full Referers | Possible Robots | Window Height |
| Time of Day | Directories | New Referers | Modem Speed | Java |
| Day of the Week | New Requests | Over Time | Platforms | Cookies |
| Month of the Year | Pages Over Time | Steps | Peak Days | Plugins |
| **Bandwidth** | **Visit** | **Problems** | **Visit Details** | **Subsets** |
| Requests by Bytes | Entry Point | Bad Links | Duration | Ads |
| Peak Hours | Exit Point | Failed Requests | Pages per Visit | Goal |
| Peak Days | Steps | Gaps in Service | Hits per Visit | User1 |
| Transfer Size | Avg View Time | Least Requested | Bytes per Visit | User2 |
| Transfer Time | Tot View Time | Reloads | Visits per Host | |
| **General** | **Paths** | **Details** | **Details** | **Custom** |
| Summary | Sources | Virtual Servers | Directory Detail | Requests One |
| Log Detail | Destinations | CGI Arguments | Methods | Requests Two |
| Configure | Paths | Auth. Users | Result Codes | Requests Three |
| Process Now | Refers To | Cookies | Agents | Referers One |
| Manual | Local Referers | File Types | Bytes by Type | Referers Two |
| **Other** | **Daily** | **Weekly** | **Monthly** | |
| Hijacking | Pages | Pages | Pages | |
| Search Engines | Downloads | Downloads | Downloads | |
| Phrase by Eng. | Graphics | Graphics | Graphics | |
| Search Logs | Others | Others | Others | |
| Modem Proxy | Requests | Requests | Requests | |
| | Refers | Refers | Refers | |

● **Summary Main Page**

Questions or comments: webmaster@gileyd.com
Copyright 1998,99,2000 by Summary.Net - Updated 4/7/00

## Hits

The thing you're probably most interested in is hits, and your software should be able to summarize them in a variety of ways. Summary Pro reports hits right in its Summary Report (see Figure 12.4), which Summary Pro also e-mails to me each time it processes the logs (I have it set to do it once a day). But I also like to review hits in the Monthly Report (see Figure 12.5) to see how site activity has changed over time.

There are different kinds of hits:

○ **PAGE HITS** are hits to Web pages—HTML documents. This is the number that should most interest you.

○ **GRAPHIC HITS** are graphics and other image files that are downloaded with Web pages. For example, if a page includes references to five graphic buttons, a logo, and a photo of your storefront, when the page is visited, there are seven graphic hits. In most cases, graphic hits should be disregarded.

○ **OTHER HITS** include other types of files that were sent from your Web server to the visitor's computer. This could include PDF files, ZIP or SIT files, style sheets (CSS files), icon (ICO) files, and any other file that is neither a page nor a graphic. You may want to disregard these hits or you may want to investigate them further to see what files site visitors are downloading. It depends on what files your site includes.

The next thing you want to know about page hits is which pages are getting hit. Your Home page *should* be getting the most hits, but it might not be. Your software should be able to break down the number of hits by page. Use this information to learn what your site visitors find most—and least—valuable on your site. You can then add more of the useful material and, if desired, remove the material that doesn't get much attention.

In Figure 12.4, you can see this information in the Content section under Pages. It's not too meaningful here because my Home page uses a frameset that references the welcome.html

FIGURE 12.4

Here's Summary Pro's Summary Report. As you can see, it's chock full of information. In case you're wondering, the gap in the Time graph is a result of me accidentally trashing 11 days worth of logs.

# SUMMARY.NET
The Next Step in Information Technology | REPORT | MENU | CONFIG |

## Summary Report

For: **wickenburg-az.com**

Calculated: Jun 02, 2000 04:54am — Including 122.05 days
From: Feb 01, 2000 12:35am — To: Jun 02, 2000 02:00am

### Time

Daily visits for the last 123 days, peak of 336 visits/day.
Hourly Report  Daily Report  Weekly Report  Monthly Report  Yearly Report
Time of Day  Day of the Week  Month of the Year

### Visitors

| | Total | Last 7 days | Avg. 7 days |
|---|---|---|---|
| Visits | 17,821 | 1,255 | 1,022 |
| Countries | 8 | | |
| Domains | 11.87% proxy.aol.com | | |
| | 9.21% uu.net | | |
| | 4.16% primenet.com | | |
| Hosts | 8.75% 208.184.159.72 | | |
| | 8.44% 12.9.138.10 | | |
| | 5.48% 207.138.23.227 | | |
| Known Robots | 44.30% HotBot Search Indexer | | |
| | 16.54% Google Search Indexer | | |
| | 7.60% Northern Light Search Indexer | | |
| Platforms | 43.01% Windows 98 | | |
| | 35.82% Windows 95/32 bit | | |
| | 11.68% (Unknown) | | |

Root Domains  Possible Robots  Modem Speed  Peak Days

### Content

| | Total | Last 7 days | Avg. 7 days |
|---|---|---|---|
| Page Hits | 35,536 | 2,719 | 2,038 |
| Downloads | 0 | 0 | 0 |
| Graphics Hits | 88,368 | 4,990 | 5,068 |
| Other Hits | 12,314 | 1,265 | 706 |
| Total Hits | 136,218 | 8,974 | 7,812 |
| Unique Requests | 565 | 364 | |
| Pages | 17.36% / | | |
| | 15.56% /welcome.html | | |
| | 13.09% /toc.html | | |
| Graphics | 5.97% /photos/windowcam01.jpg | | |
| | 5.71% /images/wickenburg-az.jpg | | |
| | 5.67% /photos/000513cowboygolf.jpg | | |

Directories  New Requests  Pages Over Time

### Referrers

| | Total |
|---|---|
| Referring Domains | 71 |
| Referring Pages | 208 |
| Referring Domains | 77.26% wickenburg-az.com |
| | 7.61% wickenburgaz.com |
| | 4.04% search.yahoo.com |
| Referring Pages | 24.86% http://www.wickenburg-az.com/welcome.html |
| | 16.22% http://www.wickenburg-az.com/ |
| | 16.13% http://www.wickenburg-az.com/toc.html |
| Search Words | 39.46% wickenburg |
| | 22.03% az |
| | 9.48% arizona |
| Search Phrases | 27.23% wickenburg az |
| | 23.36% wickenburg |
| | 13.58% wickenburg arizona |

Full Referrers  New Referrers  Over Time  Steps

### Browsers

| | Total |
|---|---|
| Browsers | 60.63% Microsoft Internet Explorer 5.x |
| | 16.95% Microsoft Internet Explorer 4.x |
| | 7.03% Netscape Navigator 3.x |

Window Width  Window Height  Plugins

### Bandwidth

| | Total | Last 7 days | Avg. 7 days |
|---|---|---|---|
| Bytes Transfered | 1,297.4M | 90,029K | 75,901K |
| Average Bits/sec | 1,156 | 1,371 | |
| Peak Hourly BPS | 7,645B 06/01/00 10 PM | | |
| | 6,604B 05/26/00 3 PM | | |
| | 6,558B 05/27/00 6 PM | | |
| Requests by Bytes | 8.63% /photos/windowcammovie.mov | | |
| | 7.26% /welcome.html | | |
| | 5.62% /photos/000513cowboygolf.jpg | | |

Peak Days  Transfer Size  Transfer Time

### Problems

| | Total | Last 7 days | Avg. 7 days |
|---|---|---|---|
| Error hits | 797 | 89 | 45 |
| Unique Failed Requests | 32 | | |
| Bad Links | 18 | | |
| Failed Requests | 54.58% /robots.txt | | |
| | 5.77% /wickenburgnewsarchive/december | | |
| | 2.51% /azresources.html | | |
| Gaps in Service | 5:11:06 May 16, 2000 02:29pm | | |
| | 2:15:57 Feb 22, 2000 04:28am | | |
| | 2:15:14 Feb 23, 2000 04:42am | | |

Least Requested  Reloads

### Visits

| | Total |
|---|---|
| Pages per Visit | 2.0 |
| Hits per Visit | 7.7 |
| Bytes per Visit | 76,043B |
| Duration of Visit | 6:22 |
| Time between Visits | 2 days 3:24 |
| Visits per host | 4.4 |
| Entry Point | 66.35% / |
| | 5.62% /welcome.html |
| | 5.27% /toc.html |
| Exit Point | 38.91% / |
| | 13.71% /gilesrd.toc.count |
| | 8.18% /styles.css |

Steps  Avg View Time  Tot View Time

### Ads

Total

### Paths

Sources  Destinations  Paths  Refers To  Local Referrers

### Details

Virtual Servers  CGI Arguments  Auth. Users  Cookies  File Types
Directory Detail  Methods  Result Codes  Agents  Bytes by Type

### Log Processing

| | |
|---|---|
| Log files | 5 |
| Log file lines | 560,259 |
| Corrupt log lines | 17 |
| Skipped log lines | 4,115 |
| Valid log entries | 556,127 |
| Filtered log entries | 76 |
| Not in any report | 0 |
| Log size in KBytes | 88,470K |
| Time to crunch | 1:51:15 |
| Log processing | 0.7 Meg/min |
| Log processing | 83 lines/sec |
| Memory used | 10,752K |
| Memory available | 5,483K |

Log Detail

**Summary Main Page**

Questions or comments: webmaster@gilesrd.com
Copyright 1998,99,2000 by Summary.Net - Updated 4/7/00

and toc.html pages. But if I click the Pages link there, I can get a list of current period page hits in order of the number of hits (see Figure 12.6).

### Referrers

Referrers are pages that site visitors were on when they clicked a link to your site. Most referrers will probably be pages on your

FIGURE 12.5
The monthly report shows basic information on a month-by-month basis. It's satisfying to see that hits have been climbing steadily—remember I lost 11 days worth of logs of April and only one day of June is included.

FIGURE 12.5
The monthly report shows basic information on a month-by-month basis. It's satisfying to see that hits have been climbing steadily—remember I lost 11 days worth of logs of April and only one day of June is included.

# SUMMARY.NET™

The Next Step in Information Technology REPORT MENU CONFIG

## Monthly Report

Shows data for the entire site during one month periods.

For: **wickenburg-az.com**
Calculated: Jun 02, 2000 04:54am  Including 122.06 days
From: Feb 01, 2000 12:35am  To: Jun 02, 2000 02:00am
Displaying items 1-5 of 5 by date.
This page as text, or spreadsheet.

| Date | Pages | Hits | Errors | MBytes | Unique Hosts | Visits | Pages |
|------|-------|------|--------|--------|-------------|--------|-------|
| February, 2000 | 5,414 | 29,099 | 103 | 256.56M | 1,162 | 2,389 | |
| March, 2000 | 9,843 | 39,504 | 169 | 387.95M | 1,359 | 4,858 | |
| April, 2000 | 5,462 | 23,804 | 128 | 243.67M | 945 | 3,587 | |
| May, 2000 | 14,333 | 42,325 | 382 | 390.10M | 1,355 | 6,787 | |
| June, 2000 | 484 | 1,486 | 15 | 14.07M | 163 | 200 | |

● Summary Main Page
Questions or comments: webmaster@gilesrd.com
Copyright 1998,99,2000 by Summary.Net - Updated 4/7/00

FIGURE 12.6
Here are the first bunch of links from the Page Requests report. It lists site pages in order of popularity. This is part of the first page of the report.

# SUMMARY.NET™

The Next Step in Information Technology REPORT MENU CONFIG

## Page Requests

Shows data about requests for pages.

For: **wickenburg-az.com**
Calculated: Jun 02, 2000 04:54am  Including 122.06 days
From: Feb 01, 2000 12:35am  To: Jun 02, 2000 02:00am
Curent period starts: May 26, 2000 02:19am
Displaying items 1-60 of 105 by hits.
This page as text, or spreadsheet.

Search: [        ] [Go]

| % of Cur Hits | Cur Hits | Cur Hits /Day | Hits /Day | Hits | First Hit | Request |
|---------------|----------|---------------|-----------|------|-----------|---------|
| 17.36% | 472 | 67.4 | 110.5 | 13,492 | 02/01/00 | / |
| 15.56% | 423 | 60.4 | 35.2 | 4,302 | 02/01/00 | /welcome.html |
| 13.09% | 356 | 50.8 | 33.5 | 4,093 | 02/01/00 | /toc.html |
| 0.00% | 0 | 0.0 | 12.4 | 1,514 | 02/01/00 | /banner.html |
| 3.75% | 102 | 14.5 | 9.6 | 1,175 | 02/01/00 | /aboutwick.html |
| 3.94% | 107 | 15.2 | 8.6 | 933 | 02/15/00 | /phototours.html |
| 1.73% | 47 | 6.7 | 6.0 | 641 | 02/16/00 | /saguarocam.html |
| 2.72% | 74 | 10.5 | 5.1 | 634 | 02/01/00 | /daytrips.html |
| 1.80% | 49 | 7.0 | 4.7 | 577 | 02/01/00 | /phototours/downtown.html |
| 1.36% | 37 | 5.2 | 3.4 | 421 | 02/01/00 | /othersites.html |
| 0.92% | 25 | 3.5 | 2.8 | 352 | 02/01/00 | /feather/ |
| 1.21% | 33 | 4.7 | 2.7 | 339 | 02/01/00 | /journal.html |
| 2.72% | 74 | 10.5 | 2.3 | 284 | 02/01/00 | /rnhomes/listings.html |
| 1.66% | 45 | 6.4 | 2.2 | 279 | 02/01/00 | /rnhomes/ |
| 2.17% | 59 | 8.4 | 9.3 | 237 | 05/07/00 | /weather/weather.html |
| 0.77% | 21 | 3.0 | 1.8 | 225 | 02/02/00 | /ranchdressings/ |
| 0.77% | 21 | 3.0 | 1.7 | 215 | 02/01/00 | /feather/gallery.html |
| 0.70% | 19 | 2.7 | 1.7 | 215 | 02/02/00 | /email.html |
| 0.63% | 17 | 2.4 | 1.6 | 195 | 02/02/00 | /phototours/wickinbloom.html |
| 2.24% | 61 | 8.7 | 1.5 | 192 | 02/01/00 | /daytrips/boxcanyon.html |
| 0.63% | 17 | 2.4 | 1.5 | 191 | 02/01/00 | /phototours/events.html |

own site, but if you have links to your site on other sites, they'll be counted, too. Links generated by search engines are also included as referrers.

In Figure 12.4, you can see some basic referrer information in the Referrers section. As you can see, 77% of the referring pages were on my own site. But 4% of the hits came from Yahoo!'s search engine. That's very comforting. The Referrer Report gives more details (see Figure 12.7) for the current period.

### Search Words & Phrases

My favorite reports are the Search Words (see Figure 12.8) and Search Phrases reports. These reports tell me what words or phrases visitors used in search engines to find my Web site. As you can see by looking closely at Figure 12.8, not everyone knows how to spell *Wickenburg*. Because I also included incorrect spellings in my keywords meta tag (as discussed in Chapter 11), bad spellers can still find my site.

**FIGURE 12.7**
The Referrer Report lists pages that site visitors were viewing when they clicked links to your site. This is only part of the report.

SUMMARY.NET
The Next Step in Information Technology [REPORT] [MENU] [CONFIG]

**Referrer Report**

Shows data about each referring page.

For: **wickenburg-az.com**
Calculated: Jun 02, 2000 04:54am  Including 122.06 days
From: Feb 01, 2000 12:35am  To: Jun 02, 2000 02:00am
Current period starts: May 26, 2000 02:19am
Displaying items 1-60 of 208 by cur hits.
This page as text, or spreadsheet.
Search: [          ] [Go]

| % of Cur Hits | Cur Hits | Hits | Pages | Down loads | First Hit | Referrer |
|---|---|---|---|---|---|---|
| 24.86% | 262 | 2,779 | 77 | 0 | 02/01/00 | http://www.wickenburg-az.com/welcome.html |
| 16.22% | 171 | 1,553 | 1,553 | 0 | 02/01/00 | http://www.wickenburg-az.com/ |
| 16.13% | 170 | 1,862 | 212 | 0 | 02/01/00 | http://www.wickenburg-az.com/toc.html |
| 3.32% | 35 | 508 | 508 | 0 | 02/01/00 | http://search.yahoo.com/bin/search |
| 3.04% | 32 | 185 | 40 | 0 | 02/16/00 | http://www.wickenburg-az.com/phototours.html |
| 2.47% | 26 | 193 | 1 | 0 | 02/05/00 | http://www.wickenburg-az.com/phototours/downtown.html |
| 2.47% | 26 | 123 | 0 | 0 | 02/14/00 | http://www.wickenburg-az.com/desertview/ |
| 2.37% | 25 | 302 | 8 | 0 | 02/02/00 | http://www.wickenburgaz.com/welcome.html |
| 1.71% | 18 | 177 | 177 | 0 | 02/02/00 | http://www.wickenburgaz.com/ |
| 1.71% | 18 | 123 | 6 | 0 | 02/03/00 | http://www.wickenburg-az.com/daytrips.html |
| 1.52% | 16 | 208 | 24 | 0 | 02/02/00 | http://www.wickenburg-az.com/toc.html |
| 1.33% | 14 | 28 | 0 | 0 | 02/23/00 | http://www.wickenburg-az.com/adventuretrails/ |
| 1.23% | 13 | 117 | 0 | 0 | 02/21/00 | http://www.wickenburg-az.com/saguarocam.html |
| 0.95% | 10 | 67 | 67 | 0 | 03/26/00 | http://aolsearch.aol.com/dirsearch.adp |
| 0.95% | 10 | 38 | 3 | 0 | 02/27/00 | http://www.wickenburg-az.com/phototours.html |
| 0.85% | 9 | 77 | 0 | 0 | 02/22/00 | http://www.wickenburg-az.com/ranchdressings/ |
| 0.85% | 9 | 73 | 73 | 0 | 04/14/00 | http://prdb.filemaker.com/poweredbyfm/FMPro |
| 0.85% | 9 | 36 | 0 | 0 | 02/10/00 | http://www.wickenburg-az.com/daytrips/boxcanyon.html |
| 0.76% | 8 | 157 | 157 | 0 | 02/02/00 | http://search.yahoo.com/search |
| 0.66% | 7 | 142 | 142 | 0 | 02/15/00 | http://www.altavista.com/cgi-bin/query |

FIGURE 12.8
The Search Words report tells me how
people search for and find my site. This
is only the first part of the report.

# SUMMARY.NET™
**The Next Step in Information Technology** `REPORT` `MENU` `CONFIG`

## Search Words

Shows individual search words used to locate this site at the major search engines. The words may have been used alone or have been part of a longer phrase.

For: **wickenburg-az.com**
Calculated: Jun 02, 2000 04:54am  Including 122.06 days
From: Feb 01, 2000 12:35am  To: Jun 02, 2000 02:00am
Displaying items 1-60 of 352 by hits.
This page as text, or spreadsheet.
Search: [          ] `Go`

| Word | % of Hits | Hits |
| --- | --- | --- |
| wickenburg | 39.46% | 1,261 |
| az | 22.03% | 704 |
| arizona | 9.48% | 303 |
| wickenberg | 4.04% | 129 |
| com | 3.10% | 99 |
| www | 1.60% | 51 |
| metasearch | 0.63% | 20 |
| in | 0.63% | 20 |
| of | 0.56% | 18 |
| ranch | 0.34% | 11 |
| wickenburgaz | 0.34% | 11 |
| city | 0.31% | 10 |
| wicken | 0.28% | 9 |
| http | 0.28% | 9 |
| community | 0.25% | 8 |
| estate | 0.25% | 8 |
| real | 0.25% | 8 |
| find | 0.22% | 7 |
| weather | 0.22% | 7 |
| wickinburg | 0.22% | 7 |
| and | 0.22% | 7 |
| virtual | 0.22% | 7 |

## Visitor Statistics

Visitor statistics tell you things about how many visitors your site had, what software they used, and how they spent their time on your site. You can see this information in the Visitor and Visits sections of Figure 12.4. Detail reports can tell you more about specific statistics.

## Errors

Although you don't want any errors in your logs, it's important that you investigate the errors that are reported. In general, errors fall into three categories:

○ **BAD LINKS ON OTHER PAGES TO PAGES ON YOUR SITE.** This can occur if a link is created incorrectly or if you moved or deleted a page that was linked to. There's not much you can do about bad links on other sites, but you can fix bad links on your own site.

- VISITORS ENTERING INCORRECT URLS FOR YOUR DOMAIN NAME. Again, this could be an error on the visitor's part or they could be trying to access a page that you've moved or deleted.

- ROBOTS OR WEB BROWSERS TRYING TO ACCESS FILES THAT DON'T EXIST ON YOUR SITE. The two biggest culprits are robots.txt (a file with instructions for search engine robots) and favicon.ico (a file referenced by Internet Explorer 5 or later when someone bookmarks your site). Neither file is required on your server and you can ignore any error messages pertaining to them if they don't exist.

### Other Information

This is just the basic information that I pay close attention to. You might find other information helpful, too. The point is, you should be monitoring your site's activity whenever possible, looking for specific, meaningful information. Only by doing this can you understand how effective your Web site is.

# Food for Thought

Ready to give some deep thought to the information in this chapter? Use the following suggestions to guide you. If you want to share your thoughts with other readers or see what other readers had to say about this chapter, visit the book's companion Web site at http://www.smallbusinessonweb.com/.

- Think about your Web site and its contents. Make a list of the pages or items that you think you'll need to update regularly.

- Take a good look at your Web site. Make a list of five features you think you might want to add in the future.

- Research some log analysis software options available to you. What kinds of reports and features do you find most important?

# Appendixes

I'm not finished yet.

Throughout this book, I listed books and Web sites that you might want to refer to as you build your Web presence. These two appendixes repeat that information right here—where it's easy to find and consult.

Keep in mind that the book's companion Web site, **http://www.smallbusinessonweb/,** provides information about additional resources that I found after the book went to print or that were suggested by readers.

# Appendixes Table of Contents

# APPENDIX A

# Bibliography

Throughout this book, I mentioned a number of other books I thought you might find helpful when building a Web presence.

In this appendix, you'll find a complete list of these books, organized by subject.

## In This Appendix

Web Publishing Books

Software How-To Books

# Web Publishing Books

# Software How-To Books

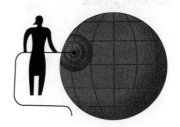

# APPENDIX B

# Web Sites & Pages

This book included references to many Web sites and pages, some presented as examples and others presented as sources of information of interest to Web publishers.

Here's a complete list of all the Web sites and pages mentioned throughout the book.

## In This Appendix

EXAMPLES

RESOURCES

# Examples

# Resources

## Book Companion Web Site

http://www.smallbusinessonweb.com/

## Basic Information

## Internet Statistics

## Search Engines

## Search Engine Information

# Index

## E

e-commerce
  barriers to, 17–18
  defined, 16
  online shopping survey, 18
e-mail
  address, including in business
    materials, 172
  contacting author via, xx
  defined, 6
  form, 93
  link, 90
  replying to, 77
  server software, 65
  signature, 174
e-retailers, profitability of, 37
eBay, 37
electronic commerce. See e-
  commerce.
Electronic Highway Robbery, 85
entertainment, using Internet for,
  17
"Error 404" message, 11, 51
error log, 200–201
Excite, 176, 185
extensions, filename, 124

## F

FAQ
  on connecting to Internet, 63
  defined, 31
  including on Web site, 78–79
fax-back service, 30
fax number, including on Web site,
  77
fax-on-demand service, 30
fee vs. free Web site, 38–40
feedback form, 96
Fenno, Richard, 133
Fetch, 165
file-naming conventions, Web
  server, 124–125
file size, and download time, 109,
  139
file transfer protocol. See FTP.
FileMaker Home Page, 130, 132–133

FileMaker Pro
  custom Web publishing
    commands, 130, 133
  and database information on the
    Web, 96, 133
  and Home Page, 130, 133
files
  limiting access to, 162–163
  naming, 124–125
  organizing, 122–124
  uploading/downloading, 6, 7,
    122, 167–169
fill-in form, 8. See also forms.
financial information, using
  Internet for, 17
firewall, defined, 7
Flash, 92
florist Web site, 113
folders
  local/remote, 122, 167
  resource, 123
  root, 123
fonts, and Windows vs. Mac
  browsers, 105
formatted text, 8, 88
forms
  database interactivity, 93–95, 97
  e-mail, 93
  guest book, 95–98
  purpose of, 8, 93
  search, 95, 96
Four "A's" marketing tool, 79–80
frame, including navbar in, 115–116
frameset, 115
free vs. fee Web site, 38–40
frequently asked questions. See FAQ.
FrontPage, 133–134
FTP
  how it works, 162
  purpose of, 6
  security features, 162–163
  software
    client, 163–165
    server, 65, 163
  uploading/updating Web site
    with, 167–169
  and Web authoring software,
    165–166, 167–168
FTP Explorer, 163–164, 168

## G

gallery, online art, 28, 29
gateway, defined, 5
GIF image format, 92
global network, Internet as
  example of, 4, 6
GoLive. See Adobe GoLive.
Gopher, 7, 8
graphic hits, and log analysis
  software, 196
graphic image
  as component of Web document,
    8, 90–93
  download times for various file
    sizes, 109
  rules for using on Web site,
    106–109
  thumbnail, 28
  Web browser-supported formats,
    92
guest book feature, 95–98

## H

Hall, C.K., 33
handouts, promotional, 26
hardware, Web server, 63–64
Harris Interactive, 13
Hester, Nolan, 134
history, Internet/Web, 5–6, 8–9
hit counter, 99–100
hits
  defined, 11
  tracking software, 65, 196–198
  types of, 196
home, accessing Internet from, 16
home-buying Web site, 23–24, 74,
  75
Home page
  defined, 11
  providing useful information on,
    113
  and Three Click Rule, 112–113,
    139
Home Page, FileMaker/Claris, 130,
  132–133
hosting. See Web hosting.
HotBot, 175

## M

Mac OS, 64
Mac OS Server, 64
Macromedia Dreamweaver,
     134–136, 166
mailing address, including on Web
     site, 77
mailing list
     purpose of, 7
     "Small Business on the Web,"
          xvii
"mailto" link, 90
maintenance. *See* site
     maintenance.
manual, product, 30
marketing activities
     contrasted with advertising and
          sales, 25
     examples of, 25–26
     importance of non-Web, 35–36
     using Web to reduce cost of,
          27–28
marketing tool, Four "A's," 79–80
markup language, 105, 120
MARQUEE tag, 105
McKinsey survey, 16
Media Metrix, 14–17
meta tags
     defined, 180
     hiding Web page with, 183
     and search engines, 181–183
     for Web site description, 180, 182
     for Web site keywords, 180–181
Microsoft FrontPage, 133–134
Microsoft Internet Explorer, 9
Microsoft Publisher, 134
Microsoft Word, 130, 134
military sites, and Internet, 5
modem, 64, 65
Mosaic, 8–9
motorcycle tour business, 27, 28,
     36, 75, 76
movies, using on Web site, 109
multimedia elements
     defined, 91
     plug-ins for, 92–93
     purpose of, 90–91, 109

tips for using on Web site, 91–93,
     109–111
types of, 109
music, using on Web site, 109,
     110–111
MyComputer.com, 14

## N

National Science Foundation
     Network, 5–6
navbar
     examples, 114, 115
     horizontal *vs.* vertical, 115
     image map, 116
     positioning, in tables *vs.* frames,
          115–116
     purpose of, 114
navigation, Web site
     breadcrumbs, 116–117
     importance of, 111–112
     with navbar, 114–117
     steps for developing, 117
     and Three Click Rule, 112–113,
          139
     tweaking, 51
navigation bar. *See* navbar.
NCSA Mosaic, 8–9
Net. *See* Internet.
.net, in Web address, 10
NetFinder, 164, 168
Netopia, 63
NetRatings, 15–16
Netscape Communications, 9
Netscape Navigator, 9
Network Solutions
     domain name registration fees,
          48
     services available from, 48, 49
     WHOIS lookup feature, 154, 155
networking software, 64
networks
     ARPAnet, 5, 6
     BITNET, 5
     corporate, 6
     DARPAnet, 5
     development of, 5–6
     illustration of, 4
     intranet, 7

LAN, 64, 65
NSFNET, 5–6
Usenet, 5
news, using Internet for, 17
newsgroup, 7
newsletter, Web-based, 39
Nielsen, Jakob, 112
Nielsen survey, 15–16
*Non-Designer's Web Book, The*, 104
Novell Netware, 64
NSFNET, 5–6
Nua Internet Surveys, 13, 14
Nuth, Bob, 23–24

## O

online chat feature, 100–101
online information, charging for,
     38–40
online shopping
     disadvantages of, 38
     offering discount for, 173
     profitability of Web sites offering,
          37
     security issues, 17, 18, 38
     survey regarding, 18
online store, contrasted with
     traditional, 37, 38
operating system software, 64
.org, in Web address, 10

## P

page hit
     counter, 99–100
     defined, 11
     tracking software, 65, 196–198
page layout, limitations of HTML
     regarding, 105
page layout program, 134
PageMill
     contrasted with GoLive, 130
     FTP features, 165–166
     recommended book on, 131
     site management features, 131
     Web authoring features, 130–132
PC-usage surveys, 13
performance issues, Internet/Web,
     11–12

permissions, copyright, 84–85
phone companies, and development of Internet, 6
phone number, including on Web site, 77
Photoshop, 131
plug-ins, 92–93
PNG image format, 92
portability, domain name, 47, 50
pricing information, including on Web site, 78
print ads
  cost considerations, 26
  including Web URL in, 173
product information
  pros and cons of various types, 25–26
  using Web to provide, 27–28, 78
product updates, 31
promotion, Web site, 172–174, 183–187
promotional handouts, 26
Publisher, Microsoft, 134
publishing features, Internet, 7. *See also* Web publishing.

## Q

QuickTime, 92

## R

real estate Web site, 23–24, 74, 75
RealPlayer, 92
reciprocating link
  defined, 91
  handling requests for, 90, 187
  looking for appropriate, 188
Referrer Report, log analysis software, 198–199
registration, domain name, 48, 49, 50, 153–154
remote copy, of Web site, 122, 167
repeat visits, encouraging, 82, 171
reports, log analysis, 195–201
research sites, and Internet, 5
resource
  contrasted with HTML document, 123

examples of, 123
file/folder, 123
moving, 126
renaming, 126
tips for avoiding problems with, 126
retailers, profitability of online, 37
revision date, including on Web site, 81
robot program, 175–176, 183, 201
Round Table Group, 15
router, 64, 65

## S

sales, contrasted with marketing, 25
sales tax, and online shopping, 38
Search Engine Watch, 174, 177, 179, 187
search engines
  adding Web site to, 183–187
  common misconceptions about, 175
  defined, 174
  how they work, 174–179
  and log analysis software, 199–200
  and meta tags, 181–183
  recommended book on, 175
  results page, 176–178
  tips for using/getting listed with, 177, 179, 185
search feature, including on Web site, 8, 95
Search Words/Phrases reports, log analysis software, 199–200
Search.com, 177–178
security
  and firewalls, 7
  and FTP server software, 162–163
  and online shopping, 17, 18, 38
server. *See* domain name server; Web server.
server co-location Web hosting, 60–62
ServerWatch, 65
setup, Web site
  choosing domain name, 47–50
  cost considerations, 45–50

shipping costs, and online shopping, 38
Shockwave, 92
shopping. *See* online shopping.
signature, e-mail, 174
SimpleText, creating Web page with, 130
simplify life, using Internet to, 16
site content. *See* content.
site design. *See also* Web designer.
  awards, 80
  consistency with other business materials, 111, 138
  cost considerations, 42–45
  developing the right look, 104–110
  do-it-yourself *vs.* professional, 42–25, 141
  navigation, 111–117
  philosophy, 148–149
  recommended books on, 104, 112
  templates and assistants, 138
site maintenance
  cost considerations, 51
  recommended activities, 51–52, 189
site management
  and Adobe PageMill, 131
  defined, 131
  and Macromedia Dreamweaver, 134–135
site revision date, including on Web site, 81
site setup
  choosing domain name, 47–50
  cost considerations, 45–50
"Small Business on the Web" companion Web site, xvii
software. *See also* specific programs.
  communications, 163
  FTP, 65, 163–165
  log analysis, 193–194
  networking, 64
  operating system, 64
  Web authoring, 130–137
  Web browser, 8–9
  Web server, 12, 64–65
software updates, 31

sound, using on Web site, 109,
110–111
spaces, in file names, 125
speed, connection, 13
spider program, 175–176
splash screen, 113–114
sports information, using Internet
for, 17
staff information, including on Web
site, 80, 81
staffing requirements, Web server,
66–67
StarNine, 193, 194
static IP address, 66
statistics, Web usage, 13–18,
192–201
store, online *vs.* traditional, 37, 38
subsite
contrasted with custom domain
name, 47–48
defined, 47
how it works, 56
portability of, 47
Summary Pro, 193, 196, 197–198
support. *See* customer support.
surfing, Internet, 13, 16
surveys, Web usage, 13–18
System Administrator, 67, 68

**T**

T1 connection, 66
table, including navbar in, 115
table of contents, Web site, 95
tags, HTML, 105, 120, 180–183
tax accountant Web site, 80
Technical contact, domain name,
154
technical documentation, 30
technical support, Web-based, 31,
78–79
telephone companies, and
development of Internet, 6
telephone number, including on
Web site, 77
templates, Web page, 138
testing, Web site, 126–127, 128,
139, 191–192

text
blinking, 105, 107
formatted, 8, 88
text editor, creating Web pages
with, 130
Three Click Rule, 112–113, 139
thumbnail image, 28
time-sensitive information,
updating, 82, 190
toll-free phone support, 30
Tollett, John, 104
tour business Web site, 27, 28, 36,
75, 76
Towers, J. Tarin, 136
TriGeo, 31–32

**U**

Uniform Resource Locator. *See* URL.
Unix, 64, 163
updating Web site, 82–83, 96, 139,
169, 190–192
uploading
defined, 6
Web pages, with FTP, 167–169
URL
adding to search engine
databases, 183–187
beginner's guide, 11
for custom domain name, 48
defined, 11
including in business materials,
172
parts of, 10–11
subsite, 47
U.S. government, and Internet, 5–6
*USA Today*, 37
usability, Web site, 112
usage logs, Web, 59, 99. *See also*
log analysis software.
usage surveys, Web, 13–18
Usenet, 5
user guide, 30

**V**

virtual domain hosting, 56, 57–59

**W**

Waddell, Dave, 27
WAIS, 7
Web. *See also* Internet; Web site.
benefits for small business
24/7 information, 22–24
image enhancement, 32–34
marketing cost savings, 24–28
support cost savings, 28–32
compatibility issues, 10
components of documents
presented on, 8
contrasted with Internet, 8
false promises regarding, 34
history of, 8–9
how it works, 9–13
size and growth estimates, 9
Web address, 10, 47. *See also*
domain name; URL.
Web analysis software. *See* log
analysis software.
Web authoring software. *See also*
specific programs.
contrasted with HTML editing,
127–130
entry-level *vs.* advanced, 130
FTP features, 165–166, 167–168
leading programs, 130–137
preview feature, 127
tips for using, 138–139
and WYSIWYG editing, 131
Web browser
defined, 9
error messages, 11
and font size, 105
history of, 8–9
how it works, 10–11
and HTML tags, 105, 120
performance issues, 11–12
and plug-ins, 92–93
testing Web site with, 126–127,
128, 139
Web consultant. *See also* Web
designer.
cost considerations, 45, 50, 52
unscrupulous, 34, 151
Web design. *See* site design.
Web Design List, 145, 146